The Book of
Rope and Knots

The Book of Rope and Knots

BILL SEVERN

Illustrated by Yukio Tashiro

David McKay Company, Inc.
New York

Reissued 1976 by the David McKay Company, Inc.
Formerly titled Rope Roundup

Library of Congress Cataloging in Publication Data
Severn, William.
    The book of rope and knots.

    First published in 1960 under title: Rope roundup.
    Bibliography: p.
    Includes index.
    1. Rope.   2. Knots and splices.   I. Tashiro,
Yukio.   II. Title.
TS1785.S38   1976   746'.04'71   76-22693
    ISBN 0-679-50691-8
    ISBN 0-679-50674-8 pbk.

MANUFACTURED IN THE UNITED STATES OF AMERICA

To
Sue and Ellen

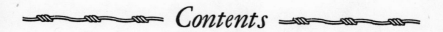

Contents

Illustrations

Full Page Diagrams

In that building, long and low,
With its windows all a-row,
  Like the port-holes of a hulk,
Human spiders spin and spin,
Backward down their threads so thin
  Dropping, each a hempen bulk.

At the end, an open door;
Squares of sunshine on the floor
  Light the long and dusky lane;
And the whirling of the wheel,
Dull and drowsy makes me feel
  All its spokes are in my brain.

As the spinners to the end
Downward go and reascend,
  Gleam the long threads in the sun;
While within this brain of mine
Cobwebs brighter and more fine
  By the busy wheel are spun.

—FROM *The Ropewalk*
BY Henry Wadsworth Longfellow

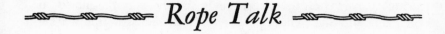 *Rope Talk*

THE WORD "rope" has different meanings for different people. When a detective "ropes" a suspect, he drops his own identity and poses as someone else to watch the person or to get information from him. But when a thief speaks of a "rope," he may be talking about a necklace and if he mentions a "milk rope," he probably means a string of pearls.

A military radar operator calls strips of tin foil dropped by parachute to confuse enemy radar reception "rope." To the tobacco salesman, the word means a bad cigar. A carnival man who gets the crowd in for a show is a "roper."

Most of us know the phrase "to rope somebody in." And when we want to give a person freedom, we say that we give him "plenty of rope." We also talk of "learning the ropes," just as the sailor does, and when we're annoyed we are often "fit to be tied." Some of us like to "spin a yarn" or to "hand somebody a line." People who marry "tie the knot" or "get hitched."

Sometimes people become "stranded." Others speak of having "frayed nerves" or being worn to a "frazzle," which is a word that means a frayed end of rope. If you get so confused that your thoughts are like a tangled ball of cord, somebody may say you are "all balled up."

We speak of a "cord of wood," which comes from the use of such a cord in measuring a quantity of cut wood. And also, of course, we talk of the "knots" in a tree. Sometimes we disrespect-fully call somebody a "knothead."

If we "string along with" a person, we follow him. But if we "string him along," we tell him an incredible story. A "second string" player is on the second team, but he may be one to "tie" the game and thus "knot the score." To the construction worker a fuse for explosives is a "string," but the cowboy calls his horses a "string."

A small-town newspaper reporter who is paid according to how much of what he writes gets printed is a "string correspond-ent," because he pastes his clippings end to end in a "string" when he sends them in to the editor to be measured so he can collect for his week's work.

Many other words and phrases in our everyday speech come from cordage and its uses. But there also are a number of spe-cialized rope terms not familiar to all of us. Some of them are listed at the end of the book under Rope Words. A knowledge of them will add to your enjoyment of this story about rope. Why not glance at the glossary now?

The Book of
Rope and Knots

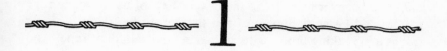

1

The Ropemakers

WHEN MAN began to walk the earth his first needs were food, shelter and clothing, but almost from the beginning, he also needed rope. Civilization would have been impossible without it and if we had no rope today, even with all our marvels of modern science, the work of the world would stop.

Man needed rope to build and hoist, haul and tie; for the boats that led him adventuring and the bridges that crossed canyons to places he had never been; to snare animals for food; to farm his crops and mine the riches of the earth. His work and often his life depended on rope, as did the outcome of his battles, the success of his trade, his transportation and his pioneering in new lands.

Because rope was among man's earliest tools, older than written history itself, most of us have come to take it for granted. Just a piece of rope, we think, something so common to all of us that it has become ordinary and unexciting. But in its making and its use lie a thousand tales and legends that reach from ancient Egypt and Greece to the China of Marco Polo, from New England's whaling ships and patriot ropemakers of the Revolution to the gold rush days of the West and the cowhand with his spinning lariat.

We all tie knots from the time we first learn to wear shoes, but many of us never learn to tie them well. Few of us who take rope for granted know the hours of fun that are to be found in doing things and making things with an inexpensive length of rope. And we seldom realize how much we really depend on rope in our day-to-day lives.

Pull open the drapes of your living room window or raise the Venetian blinds, lift the sash if you live in an older house, and you need cord to do it. Look out the window and see a girl skipping rope, a housewife at the clothesline, boys using rope to climb a backyard tree or to swing beneath its limbs. The hammock between the trees is held by rope and if you get out the power mower to cut the grass, you will need rope to start it.

Turn on the TV and remember that rope may have been needed to hoist the antenna to the roof; switch on the record player and the violin music you hear comes from strings; tie a package to mail and it takes cord. The roast of meat in the refrigerator has been tied by a butcher who is a practised hand with string and knots.

Down the street, a shopkeeper lowers his awning with cord and the flag in front of the school is raised on its halyard. A steeplejack at the church slings his bo'sun's chair to paint the steeple where bells will chime on Sunday to the pull of rope. Trucks rumble along the street, bringing all the things we eat and wear and use, their cargoes lashed with rope.

Builders, painters and riggers use tons of rope to put up new homes and skyscrapers and to fix over the older ones, to hoist heavy equipment into windows far above the ground. The bridgebuilders and other high-construction men depend on rope safety nets as they walk their narrow girders of steel. Rope is the life line as well as the tool of the linemen who brave storms and winter ice to climb telephone and utility poles.

Millions of pounds of rope are used every year by farmers for

tie lines, halters, tow lines, plow lines, blocks and tackle, as well as millions more pounds of twine for tying and binding wheat, hay and other crops. Ships, even in these days when sails are gone except for sport, need half a hundred different kinds of rope in addition to the nets and slings to load and unload everything from bananas to elephants for a zoo.

The fisherman, miner, quarryman, oil well driller, circus performer, lumberman, theater stage hand and the workers in some four hundred other types of jobs couldn't get along without ropes. When we take a winter vacation, there are ski ropes to pull us up a snowy crest and, in the summer, another kind of rope for water skiing or as safety lines for swimming. Jet plane targets are towed through the sky by nylon cord; ranger troops climb cliffs and buildings with their toggle ropes; parachutists, tumbling out to earth, depend on their rip cords to let them float safely down.

Rope has been made of many things—hides and hair, vegetable fibers and the bark of trees, cotton, wire, coconuts and silk. But probably the first ropes weren't made at all. They just grew, in the form of twisted tendrils of vines.

Man found that the twisted strands were stronger and could be wound into longer lengths than the single, untwisted cords of primitive materials he had been using. The vine ropes were a product of nature, like fire, that man discovered and later learned to adapt to serve his needs.

Nobody really knows when or where he first decided to twist or braid strands together and create man-made rope. Some say that Adam may have learned the lesson from braiding Eve's long hair. But the scientific guess is when man developed as a hunter and a fisherman in his search for new sources of food, he was no longer content with a single cord of vegetable fiber or an unplaited thong of hide. So, necessity being as always the mother of invention, he made rope.

At any event, he was putting rope to many uses long before he thought of using logs as wheels to move things too heavy for lifting by hand. When he also learned, centuries later, to put the rope over a crude wheel and thus invent the pulley, civilization took a giant step forward.

But in the early days, starting with vines, man made use of whatever ropemaking materials he could find in his part of the world. Even when there was no plant life around him, he managed to find some material that could be made into rope. When he migrated, he carried his crafts and products with him and found raw materials in the new areas he settled.

Ropemaking was known even in the remotest places, discovered by separate tribes as they emerged from savagery. It was a universal skill, possibly from the time man first swung from trees, bound his enemy, or wove a net across the entrance to his cave to keep out wild animals.

Braided rope of animal hide was made in southwest Asia before 4000 B.C., and not long afterwards other ancient Asiatics made twisted rope by rolling bark fibers together with the palm of the hand on the bare thigh. Braiding and twisting remain the methods of ropemaking today. Generally, soft fiber cords, such as cotton, are now braided and hard fiber ropes are twisted.

The first method led to mat making, basket making and true weaving and the second to spinning and thereby gave us not only rope, but also the basic processes by which textiles were made. Thus, to the early ropemakers, we might give our thanks that we wear suits and dresses of cloth instead of animal skins.

We know rope was made in southeastern Europe in 3000 B.C., because some of the pottery of that period has patterns that were formed by pressing spun cord into the clay. And heavy rope must have been in common use in the Mediterranean area about a thousand years later since the busy ships of that time couldn't have operated without it.

Some 3,500 years ago, the Egyptians had a ropemaking technique that is still followed in basic method by the machines that manufacture rope today. A wall painting on a tomb at Thebes shows how stems of papyrus grass that grew in the swamps of the

Nile were beaten to fiber and how the fibers were spun into yarns, formed into strands and laid into rope.

Mallets were used for the beating and whirling tools for spinning. Each tool had a handle to which was shackled a stick with a weight on the end for momentum, so the spinner could twist his yarns by whirling it as he walked backward. His helper sat holding a spike between the strands against a similar spike stuck in the ground and another figure is shown laying the twisted strands into rope.

The Egyptians used rope of papyrus, and also of camel hair, to moor small ships in harbor, tie animals, lift water from deep wells and to pull the stones that built their temples and age-enduring pyramids. Egyptian big game hunters, sporting on the Nile Delta, used thick ropes and harpoon-like spears to hunt the hippopotamus from boats of balsa reed that were lashed together with papyrus cord.

Ropemaking in ancient India was so specialized that one class of experts made rope just for horses and another for elephants. The early Chinese had elaborate ceremonial ropes of silk. Sculptures of Greece and Rome show gangs of men pulling cables to lift the columns of towering monuments. And undoubtedly, if the face of Helen of Troy was beautiful enough to launch a thousand ships, as legend has it, those ships also needed rope.

Without rope, Persia's mighty ruler, the great king Xerxes I, might never have conquered the Greeks. Xerxes, who is referred to in the Bible as Ahasuerus, led his Persian warriors to their empire-building victories some 2,400 years ago by what then seemed the impossible task of bridging a mile-wide waterway that his enemies were sure troops would never cross except by ship.

He had already brought Egypt under Persian rule when he planned the bold military strategy for the invasion of Greece. The Greeks felt well-protected by the swirling waters of the Hellespont, which was what the strait of the Dardanelles was then called. If the invaders came, they would have to cross in boats that could bring ashore only small groups of warriors at a time. But Xerxes hit on a plan to pour all his invading troops on land at once.

It called for cutting a canal through the isthmus of Athos and then constructing a bridge across the Hellespont. Nobody then, of course, had ever built a bridge that long, but Xerxes planned a different kind of bridge. He led his armies to Abydos, where the strait reached its narrowest point, but was still a broad current that separated him from the distant shore with waters that ran at a pull of about three miles an hour.

With two Phoenician-made ropes of white flax and four other ropes of Egyptian papyrus, called biblos, the Persians lashed together a bridge of boats and barges. The six miles of rope held the string of boats in their temporary bridge, some of the cables being of enormous size, while Xerxes' armies swarmed across.

They marched through Thrace and Macedonia, to victory over brave Leonidas and his Spartans, and finally occupied Athens.

Homer frequently mentioned rope in the Odyssey and so did Vergil in the Aeneid. The great biblical strong man, Samson, hinted to Delilah, when she asked the secret of his powerful strength, that if he were tied up in brand-new rope he might not be able to break his bonds and escape. "If thou only bind me with new ropes wherewith no work has been done," he told her, "then shall I become weak."

Ropes made from the fiber of yew trees held together the hewn-oak planks of boats used by the ancient Britons 400 years before Julius Caesar and there were established ropemakers in England during the Roman invasion. Even before that time, mechanical techniques probably had improved to the point where hand-manufacture included the use of a crank-turned spinner for forming the strands.

By the 13th century, ropemaking was a common trade in England. The first ropers' guilds were formed there about one hundred years later, when ropes were being used in pit mining. Medieval monks had long been making ropes to ring bells and for cinctures to tie around their waists. The gatekeepers of the castles of Northern Europe often lifted their drawbridges with rope to keep out the marauding bands who clattered on horseback to their moats.

But it was the burgeoning age of sailing ships that brought ropemaking into its own. Sails made rope a vital industry, because without it there could be no great vessels to voyage the Seven Seas in search of the far-off lands of trade. Rigging was essential to the ships in which Columbus and the other great navigators made their voyages of exploration and discovery of the New World.

Ages before the Spaniards came, however, rope was common throughout all the Americas. The prehistoric Incas of Peru, who developed a decimal system of knotted cords as a substitute for writing, made excellent ropes of the fibers of the maguey at least as long ago as the ancient Egyptians. Inca ropes were strong enough to support primitive suspension bridges across the plunging gorges of the Andes.

They and other Indians also used the long, stout tendrils of the wild grapevine, twisted or braided into strands, for bridges that carried humans and heavily-loaded animals. Sometimes small logs or slats were bound and suspended with rope and at other times, among more primitive tribes, a "bridge" was only a long vine cable tied to a high tree so a man could swing out on it across a river and drop himself safely down at the other side.

Central America's highly civilized Mayas used rope made of henequen from Yucatan to haul huge blocks of stone from the quarries and to lift them into place in building their magnificent ancient temples of idol worship. Mexican Indians of a later date used two small tree branches, stuck in the ground and trimmed so as to leave forks at the top, for ropemaking. Two stone wheels on stick axles were placed, one above the other, across these upright branches and the Indian twisted the cord from his hands through the wheels.

A favorite ropemaking material among various tribes of our own North American Indians was the inner bark of the basswood tree. They pulled long and narrow strips of bark from the tree and soaked them in water for a week so as to separate the inner bark easily from the rough outer layer. After bending the layers apart, they ran a fingernail down the edge to get tiny strips and then boiled those in a lye solution of wood ashes and water to make them more pliable.

The fibers were pulled back and forth over a smooth pole until they separated into fine threads. An Indian, seated on the ground, made twine of these by putting two thin threads on his thigh and rolling them toward his knee with the palm of his hand. When he came to the end of the pieces he was twisting, he cut off one thread shorter than the other and spliced in a new one, so that none of the threads ended at the same spot as another. He could thus twist a strong twine into any length he desired.

He made his light and smooth basswood rope by hanging damp bunches of strands over a peg or a tree crotch and taking a bunch in each hand so as to twist them in opposite directions as he laid the strands together. When he had added enough strands to make the rope as long as he wanted it to be, he took it from the peg and stretched it between two trees. Several times a day, he would unfasten it and stretch it tight again, allowing it to dry and cure.

The inner bark of elm, hickory, white oak, red cedar and mulberry trees was made into Indian rope in much the same way. Sometimes the whole bark of the leatherwood and pawpaw was peeled from young shoots, ready to use. Indians also used hemp, dried stalks of nettle, the fiber of purple-flowered swamp milkweed, the leaves of the yucca of the southwestern desert, the roots of hemlock, pine and cottonwood.

Horsehair ropes were common among the Indians of the South-west and others made cord of animal hide and sinews. The sinews were cut from buffalo, moose, deer and elk and hung to dry in a state in which they could be kept almost indefinitely. When cord was needed, the Indians wet the sinews and pounded them until the fibers separated into threads. Hide was cut into strips, split and scraped. Sometimes the Indians chewed it to make it soft.

Indian ropes often were braided instead of being twisted, the hanks of fiber being hung from a tree and plaited much in the manner that a girl would comb and braid long hair. Other tribes used crossed wooden sticks, lateral poles or the toes of their feet to keep the strands separate while braiding them.

Whale-hunting tribes of the northwest coast, who took to sea in forty-foot log canoes, made their whaling lines of an unusual cedar rope that looked somewhat like the ropes we use today. They twisted small branches into three-strand rope that was four to five inches around and sometimes more than a thousand feet long.

But the first colonists in Virginia and the Pilgrims who came to Plymouth had no access to Indian ropes and the very ships that brought them also brought the immediate need for rope. There wasn't nearly enough imported to meet demands. Crude cordage was made at the start, both in Virginia and New England, by some of the settlers themselves. They hand-twisted it in the fields for their own uses, but family-made rope supplied only a small part of what was needed.

Within fifteen years of the Pilgrim landing, Joseph and Philip Veren went into the business of making rope by setting up ropewalks in Salem, Massachusetts, in 1635. Some five years later, when the first ship was being built at Boston, an expert ropemaker, John Harrison, was brought from Salisbury, England, to make rigging for it and to serve the other colonists.

The vessel which he equipped with rope to sail forth from the new America and to bring back to Boston fruit, linen, oil and wool from the ports of trade was the 160-ton *Trial*. Harrison's rope was made in a walk he set up in the field adjoining his house at the foot of Summer Street in a Boston then only a small village. The walk was a straight strip of ground, along which he set posts so as to hang his strands as he backed down it, paying out hemp fiber through his hands.

Harrison had come to Boston with the understanding that nobody else would be allowed to enter the ropemaking business to compete with him and he kept his monopoly for years, settling down in the colony to prosper and to raise a family of eleven children. Even in his old age, when another man wanted to make fishline, not rope, Harrison complained that it would cut his income, so the town fathers withdrew the other man's permit. But, although Harrison was able to keep competition out of Boston, other ropewalks quickly sprang up in the surrounding areas.

Money was scarce in the new colonies and the founders, almost from the beginning, urged people to raise and harvest wild hemp, not only for their own rope needs but also as a crop to export to the ropemakers of England so as to get cash to settle debts for other imported goods. The colonists had great expectations for the wild grass that had long been used by the Indians for rope. Samples of it were declared far better than English hemp.

The General Court of Massachusetts pointed out in 1640 that the worthwhile sum of two pence was being offered for each pound of hemp and enjoined the people to work their children and their servants "early and late" to gather it. Two years later, the Connecticut Court ordered everyone having hemp seed to sow it or to sell it to others for sowing "to better furnish the River" with cordage for ship rigging.

Massachusetts stepped up the campaign in 1701 by chartering a company to buy all good hemp at a fixed price, to which a bounty was added and paid to the company out of the public treasury. The bounty was later increased and New Hampshire, meanwhile, declared that hemp would be accepted from growers in exchange for taxes. But despite all this encouragement, most hemp was still imported during the early years.

Ropemaking was a regular pursuit throughout the colonies by around 1700. Most of the ropewalks were along the seacoast, since the demand for manufactured rope was mainly for shipping and fishing. The need was so great that in the years prior to the Revolution fourteen ropewalks were all spinning busily at the same time in Boston alone. Portsmouth, New Hampshire, had three, and there was at least one in nearly every settlement of any size. Ropemaking had become a principal branch of Colonial industry.

Many of the early ropewalks were no more than outdoor fields like Harrison's, a quarter-mile of flat meadow or pasture land where rope was produced in a way that had gone almost unchanged for centuries. Marked out by a series of pegged posts to hold the rope hung over them as it was made, these were factories with only the sky for a roof and the earth for a floor. But it wasn't long before the ropewalks took cover to escape the interruptions of the weather.

They then became narrow sheds, more than a thousand feet long and perhaps thirty feet wide, so that three or four rope-makers could work side by side at the same time. Along the sides, there were square open windows that let the boxed rays of the sun into the tunnel-like space that was filled with the rattle and whirr of wooden cranks, the tinkle of bells and the pungent smell of hot tar.

Before hemp reached the ropewalk, it was processed in the field by drawing the harvested plants through spikes at the end of a plank to extract the fiber and then under saw-toothed knives mounted on flat tables.

When it was brought to the ropemaker's mill, workers beat the fiber to soften it and make it more pliable. This was done at a series of fairly wide and waist-high upright wooden posts with

semi-circular slots at the tops through which the fiber could be drawn while men flailed it with paddles that looked somewhat like English cricket bats.

Then it had to be combed to remove snarls and short fibers, the iron-peg combs being spaced at intervals on the surface of a "hackle" board, erect metal prongs like the hair of a cat or dog with its "hackles up." The fiber was pulled by hand through the hackling combs until it was ready for spinning into yarn.

Rope, then as now, was made by a series of opposite twists. If the yarns and strands were turned all one way, they would untwist themselves and part at the slightest strain. But by turning each in opposite ways, the ropemaker took advantage of their tendency to untwist and the result was a firm cord bound together by the friction of its parts.

If you take a piece of standard hard-fiber rope apart, you will find it usually has three strands. Unlay one of the strands and you will find a number of yarns. If you untwist one of the yarns, you will see the many fibers. Standard rope is made in three twisting operations that start with *spinning* these fibers from left to right to make the yarn. Several yarns are then twisted together the opposite way, from right to left, to *form* a strand. Three or more strands next are turned together from left to right to *lay* the rope.

In the old ropewalks, the spinning was done with a wheel that stood at one end of the walk. This was connected to a dozen or so rollers, in each of which a metal hook was mounted. When a helper, usually a young boy learning the trade, cranked the wheel, the rollers revolved and set the hooks spinning. One boy at the crank could supply the power to spin a number of yarns at the same time.

But feeding the hemp into each separate yarn required the expert skill of a man at the other end. He was the spinner, whose practiced fingers counted for far more than what the wheel could do. The spinner would take a bunch of hackled hemp fiber, wind it many times around his waist so that the bundle had an opening to the front, and then hook a loop of a few fibers over one of the hooks of the wheel.

As the helper cranked the wheel, the spinner would walk backward from it, slowly down the length of the ropewalk, carefully letting out the fiber from his waist like a human spider. His right hand, covered with a woolen cloth, payed out the hemp between his fingers, compressing it and keeping it to an even size, while his left hand fed more fibers smoothly into the twisting yarn.

With gestures, or the tinkle of an overhead bell, he let the boy helping him know how fast to turn the wheel to regulate the twist of the yarn. Above the spinner's head, fixed in wooden crosspieces about thirty feet apart, were hooks for him to toss the spun yarn over as he passed, so as to keep it from sagging to the ground.

After several hundred of the hempen yarns had been spun, they were bundled into a batch called a "haul," slightly twisted together, and dipped into a kettle of bubbling hot tar, needed to protect the yarn from weather and the salt of the seas. The batch was then dragged through the hole of a metal disc to press the tar into the yarn and remove the surplus.

Several tarred yarns were formed into strands, by a backward-walking and wheel-turning process much the same as the spinning of the yarns, and the strands finally were laid into rope in their last opposite twisting. In the old days, the maximum length of one coil of rope depended on the length of the ropewalk. Because of the twisting, the finished rope was shorter than the individual strands that went into it.

Rope that came from the same walk often was of different quality from one day to the next because so much depended on the experience and skill of the men involved, not to mention the mood a ropemaker might happen to be in on any particular day. If he had an off day when he felt weary or wasn't paying strict attention to his job, or if his fingers were numbed by the freezing wintry cold of the unheated shed, a poor coil of rope might result.

It was a credit to the skill of the ropemakers that so much of what they produced was excellent.

They were artisans, most of them, but also rough and hardy men. Often, they worked in near-zero temperatures and when the walks were shut down because of the cold, it wasn't so much for their comfort as because the tarred yarns were too stiff to work into strands of rope. In Boston, at least, the ropemakers had a reputation as boisterous fellows who dearly loved a fight.

It was a series of scraps between Boston's ropemakers and British soldiers stationed there in 1770 that touched off the historic "Boston Massacre," which inflamed feelings throughout the colonies in the period leading up to the Revolutionary War.

The redcoats had been sent in to keep peace among the rebellious Bostonians and to enforce the hated Townshend Acts for the collection of customs duties. Boston scorned and insulted the soldiers at every opportunity and the redcoats, their tempers on edge, returned the hostility.

With feelings running high, a number of free-for-all fights among soldiers and ropemakers led to a mass demonstration against the British in which troops fired on a band of fifty or sixty people who were pelting them with snowballs. Amid the wild confusion, five Bostonians were mortally wounded and six others hurt. One of the ropemakers was among the casualties. Word of the shooting aroused emotions in all the colonies as no dry talk of politics could and brought many people rallying to the cause of Revolution.

Ropemaking, like almost all Colonial commerce, was hard hit by the Revolution, but while some ropewalks were closed by the occupation of cities, or lack of manpower and materials, new ones opened. Despite their hardships, the ropemakers managed to supply some rope to the armies and, more importantly, to the vital ships at sea which couldn't move without it.

The first heavy American losses at sea soon were replaced by larger vessels which needed even more rope. Coastal skippers became captains of fleets as merchants converted their ships of trade into floating arsenals that went privateering. The privateers, which were privately owned vessels of war commissioned to capture enemy shipping, were largely manned by what had been peaceful fisherfolk and sailors. Coastal ports boomed with activity as the privateers set out to seize hundreds of British ships and the sorely-wanted supplies they carried as cargo.

Boston alone had 365 vessels commissioned to international piracy, little Rhode Island over 200, and the legal pirates operated in the cause of patriotism, as well as profit, from nearly every port or inlet deep enough to give them harbor. While occasional coils of finished rope, as well as hemp for ropemaking, were among the prizes seized from the British ships, the ropewalks worked from early dawn until it became too dark to see, serving the privateers with the lines for their rigging.

When the war ended and union had been achieved, it was the skippers and owners of the privateers who led the opening of the great shipping trade with China and India and thus created a demand for more rope than ever before. From then until well after the Civil War, sailing ships were the biggest business of the ropemakers. And all the knots and crafts of rope were, of course, the major skill of the sailor.

Americans, right after the Revolution, were hungry for imported goods that had been cut off by the war. Ordinary commerce with Europe and the West Indies was resumed as soon as peace was sure. Coastal ships ranged from Maryland, Virginia and the Carolinas to the lumber ports of the North to collect natural products for shipment overseas aboard vessels that would bring back the imports which other coastal ships, in turn, could deliver to cities such as New York and Philadelphia.

Since there were yet no railroads, most passengers and local freight also went from one American city to another by ship. There is no way to guess the amount of rope consumed by all the shipping, but it must have been enormous, since one large vessel alone, completely rigged, might use nearly a mile of rope. In later years, when sailing ships were still larger, some of them needed two miles of cordage in sizes from two to nine inches, plus about a ton of smaller lines.

Yankee captains from the port of Salem were pioneers of the China trade that began in the 1790's, sailing their ships around the ends of the earth to bring back rich and exotic goods from Asia to the simple townsfolk, fishermen and corn-planters of the new United States. Their voyages of eighteen months or more often followed a great triangular course, from New England around the tip of South America, up the Pacific to the Northwest, and then to China and back to Boston.

For six months before a Canton ship left Salem, a small fleet of brigs and schooners would ply about getting her cargo ready. They brought iron, hemp and duck from Sweden and Russia, wine and lead from France and Spain, rum and sugar from the West Indies. Into the holds of the Orient-bound ship also went native products, flour, fish, iron and tobacco. Sometimes, there would be fur from the Indians to carry to the Chinese in Canton. The Salem skippers brought back coffee, tea, silk and muslins and occasionally jewels, jade or teakwood furniture.

Whalers were good customers of the ropemakers, too, but it took them awhile to recover from the ruin that the Revolution had caused their business. Long wartime privation had taught families to avoid expensive whale oil and to make their own tallow light for their homes. But the whaling business was given a big boost around 1788 when the number of lighthouses increased and brought a need for sperm oil that encouraged the whalers.

New Bedford, which had lost its whale ships in the Revolution, went back into the business with a drive that before many years took over three-fourths of the whale fishery of the country and made it the biggest whaling port on earth. Following the example of the skippers of the China Trade, the whalers began to pursue their Moby Dicks in the far reaches of the Pacific.

The typical whaler of 1791 carried a crew of seventeen, so as to man three smaller whaleboats with five men each, while two men stayed aboard the whaler as "keepers of the ship" when the others were on the hunt. Whalers used a lot of rope aside from the ordinary standing and running rigging. They had to carry replacements for their long months of cruising the Pacific, voyages that sometimes took them away from New Bedford for as much as three years.

While the peak decade of whaling didn't begin until 1835, when there were more than seven hundred American ships in the trade to supply the nation with oil, whalers consumed hundreds of fathoms of whale warp even in the earlier years. That was the line, payed out from the tubs of the whaleboats, that was attached to the harpoons. It took the finest grade of hemp and expert rope-makers to produce whale warp. When the loss of a whale or even a man's life was at stake, no chances could be taken that the line might kink or snap apart.

Only the best of ropes also were used aboard the famous clipper ships that were built first in Baltimore and then in Boston. Long and narrow and designed for speed, with a bow that cleaved the waves, those fastest of all sailing ships carried a cloud of sails and a mighty gang of rope. They steadily cut the time needed for long voyages, had famous races, and dominated commerce to far places of the world, to China and Australia, and around the Horn to California in the later gold rush days.

The clippers started in the 1830's, but really came into their own after steamships were already crossing the ocean, easily outrunning the slow steam vessels at first. By around 1860, the improved steamships began to forge ahead. Some of the fastest clippers were built after that, but the golden age of the sailing ship was then dying away. Such a thing, a time without sails, was not within the remote imagination, however, of the ropemaker busily supplying the men of the sea who were building America's great new shipping trade after the Revolution.

Sailors aboard the old sailing ships timed the pulling of their ropes to the singing of traditional songs and measured chants that helped them with their work. They had what were called "pulling songs" and "windlass songs." Some came from the seafaring days of England while others were made up by the American mariners as they went about their labors, improvised folk songs that took their rhythm from the hauling in of the ropes.

The pulling songs, sung in chorus by the men working a sail rope, had the very practical use of helping a crew all pull on the line together at the exact instant a certain note was sounded. Without that precise timing of many hands and arms in unison, the mighty sails would have been too heavy to raise.

Some of the pulling songs had only a single chorus, sung over and over until the sail was up. One of the popular chants was:

Way, haul a-way, haul a-way, my Joe-sie.
Way, haul a-way, haul a-way, Joe.

Another one the men often sang was part of a ballad about someone named Jean François. The rest of it must have been forgotten since only the chorus was chanted to the pulling of the rope:

> *Oh, drive her, cap-tain, drive her!*
> *Way-a-yah!*
> *Oh, drive her, cap-tain, drive her!*
> *To my Johnnie Fran-swaw.*

Windlass songs were sung while hauling up the anchor rope, working pumps or loading and unloading ships with rope slings, to give spirit to the work of routine jobs that could be made less boring if the time were passed in the comraderie of song. Usually, they were far more elaborate than the pulling songs, with many verses that told a legend of the seas or of the sailor's longing for home.

A blundering sailor called "Randso" was among the comic characters of one windlass song that went on in an endless number of verses about his faults:

> *Oh, Rand-so was no sail-or.*
> *Ah, Randso, boys, ah, Randso.*
> *He shipped on board of a whaler.*
> *Ah, Randso, boys, ah, Randso.*
> *He could not do his duty*
> *So they gave him nine-and-thirty*
> *Ah, Randso, boys, ah, Randso.*

Before the coming of steam, with the hiss and clank and rattle of machinery that silenced the rope-pulling sailors by making song impossible over the noise, the boss of the deck crew was the bard of the forecastle.

He was the one who had the hundreds of rope-working songs at the tip of his tongue, ready to cue the men by singing the first chorus to them and giving each verse in solo for the sailors to chime in. He varied the melody, added little vocal tricks, set the gay or melancholy mood and always was careful to rest his own voice while the others sang.

Sometimes he made up new verses as he went along to josh the men or to comment in rhyme on happenings aboard the vessel. There were songs about the rope itself, such as a vocal complaint against the bowline that had to be hauled "so ear-ly in the mornin'." During the war with England in 1812, the singing of some of the English rope pulling songs was forbidden on American ships, or words were changed to those considered more patriotic.

By 1810, the cordage needs of the young United States had swelled the number of the country's ropewalks to 173. The larger cities, while admitting the need for rope, weren't always glad to have the walks within city limits. Because of the use of tar in treating the hemp, and because the rambling long frame sheds frequently were prime fire hazards in themselves, there were many serious fires which destroyed property and caused alarm.

Several cordage plants and ropewalks burned down on a cold February day in 1797 in West Boston, causing a $100,000 loss. After three other big Boston fires, ropewalks that were located at what is now the city's Public Garden were moved out to the suburbs in 1819. In 1837, the Franklin Hemp and Flax factory burned. Officials in other cities began to pass regulations to move the walks into less populated sections.

There were smaller ropewalks serving rural areas with farm ropes, well ropes and halters for animals, but in the 1800's nearly every well-regulated farm made its own rope of flax. The flax was pulled in the field, bound into bundles, soaked in a nearby brook or pond, and left to dry in the sun before being worked so the fiber could be separated from the rotted outer straw covering.

Flax was used on the farm to make many things from fine linen to coarse work breeches. During the combing out of the fiber, great snarls and twists were left and this by-product, that just naturally accumulated, was known as "tow."

The women of the household took the good flax fiber to make linen thread on the familiar parlor spinning wheel. This, incidentally, gave us the word "spinster" for an unmarried woman who supposedly sat at home spinning yarn for her wedding clothes. The left-over tow was stored in loose sacks in a shed loft until "rope-making time" on the farm, usually in the early spring.

The farmer's wife and two daughters, or maybe a neighbor's daughter who came over to help for the day, made the rope. There were spindles on which to fasten the end strands of the tow. Each woman would toss an open sack, filled with the tow snarls, over her shoulder and tie it at her waist. Then she would walk backward, paying out the right amount, much as she had learned to do with her spinning wheel, twisting it and keeping it taut.

Now and then, she would pause to wet the forming rope with a sprinkle or two from a nearby oaken water bucket to keep it pliable. As she backed down the cow lane she, or one of her helpers, would tie every four feet of the rope with a small string of tow called a "twitchet," until the desired length was reached. The rope usually was very crude and tended to pull apart rather easily, but it served many farm uses.

Boys taken on as apprentices at the commercial ropewalks in the early 1800's usually started to learn the trade when they were about sixteen. They had to sign indentures, promising to serve the master faithfully, to obey his every command, to keep out of trouble in their off-hours and not to play cards, gamble or get married. For this, they were given their room, board and spending money of about thirty-five dollars a year.

When they came of age at 21, if they had served their master well, they could have regular factory jobs. But ropemaking was such hard work, many boys ran away without serving out their apprenticeships, some of them shipping off for adventure at sea. Those who stayed on and became spinners at the ropewalks could expect wages of a little more than a dollar a day, and in those times the work-day was from sunrise to sunset, Monday through

Saturday, with four holidays a year. But their rent for a home was only a dollar a week and meat for the table cost ten cents a pound.

The ropemakers resisted the coming of machinery to replace the skilled operations they had so long done by hand. Many of the owners were against it on the grounds that machines were too costly and unnecessary. And the ship captains, who were their best customers, also were against any change in the traditional making of rope, arguing that no machines could turn out a product as good as that hand-made to their exact needs.

But the enormous growth of sailing, the coming of new fibers not so easily spun by hand, and the price-cutting competition which put so many smaller ropewalks out of business and forced those remaining to increase their output, gradually brought the change to machines. However, in some places, the old long sheds and the sensitive hands of the rope spinners held on in traditional ways until well after the Civil War.

Hemp was the usual fiber of rope in the early 1800's. It was a soft material that could be hand-spun with ease. Smooth, creamy-tan Russian hemp, then preferred by most seamen, was brought by ship from the Baltic. Dark gray American hemp was produced in quantity mainly in Kentucky and the upper Mississippi Valley. Tar for it came in barrels from North Carolina.

When Lieutenant John White of the U.S. Navy brought a sample of abaca to Salem from the Philippines in 1820, rope-makers quickly realized it was superior to hemp. They began importing it from Manila and the fiber, from a plant that is a cousin to the banana plant, took the name of that port city. Manila fiber made a rope that was cleaner and more durable, had far greater stretch and strength, and didn't have to be tarred to protect it from moisture, heat and the salt of the sea as hemp was.

Sailors found the new manila rope easy on their hands, quick to dry and to coil without kinking, lighter in weight to put aloft, longer lasting and more dependable. Whalers, who had to risk their lives on their towlines, were eager to get it for their whaling warp. Soon nearly everybody was demanding it and imports from the Philippines leaped by tons until manila became the main fiber of the ropemaking industry.

The first machinery in the ropewalks merely substituted the power of horses or water for some jobs done by hand. Some of the work of hand-cranking was given over to horses that plodded a well-worn circle behind the rope shed, hitched to a huge driving beam which clanked around great iron cogwheels. The constant rumbling, squeaking and building-shaking clatter, and the choking dust that came up on hot summer days from the hooves of the rounding horses, often got on the nerves of the men who were against such new-fangled ways. Three or more horses were worked in rotation and often pressed into extra service to pull the wagons that delivered rope to customers.

Where there was a swift stream or a strong tidal inlet, power might be supplied to the forming and laying of the rope by a water wheel. This was attached to a shaft and belted by an endless rope to the driving wheel of a low platform-like car that ran the length of the walk on rails. The platform had a machine on it to strand the yarns through a tube or twist the strands into rope, moving slowly backward as the ropemakers previously had afoot. But the initial process of spinning the fiber into yarn usually was still done by hand.

The coming of steam power brought an outburst of ropemaking inventions. Dr. Edmund Cartwright, who revolutionized the textile industry by inventing the power loom, also gave ropemakers one of their basic machines.

He was an English clergyman, rector of a country parish, when he became interested in the possibility of applying machinery to weaving. By 1785, he had patented the first crude contrivance that he later developed as the power loom, which helped bring about the great Industrial Revolution. Cartwright was somewhat ahead of his times and failed financially when he started his first textile factory. Another mill he operated was set afire.

But he continued his inventions and patented a ropemaking machine in 1792. This was the industry's basic steam-powered twisting machine, called a cordelier. Cartwright exchanged ideas about it with other inventor friends, including Robert Fulton of steamboat fame, who was then working on a ropemaking device of his own.

Daniel Treadwell of Boston, who applied steam power to the printing press, invented a spinning jenny for rope yarn that was introduced into the Charlestown Navy Yard in 1836. Inventor Moses Day developed a steam machine that replaced the need of a boy to turn the spindles, thus saving space and doing away with the services of the skilled apprentice. An unskilled worker could sit within a comfortably heated building and let the machine spin out manila yarn.

The ropemakers still lagged behind the spinners of cotton and woolen yarn in their readiness to take to machines. But the nation was growing inland as well as along the coast. The new canal systems and the start of railroads, the whole push of commerce and settlement, needed rope in greater lengths and quantities than the ropewalks could turn out by hand.

The first boat went through New York's Erie Canal from Rome to Utica in October, 1819, to the stirring music of a band, the ringing of bells and a salute of roaring cannon. Described by newspaper accounts as an "elegant craft" with two rising cabins and a flat deck between them, it was called the *Chief Engineer*.

Aboard were the governor and other dignitaries to celebrate the opening of the inland water route that was to make the state the gateway for travelers to the West. Drawn at a speed of a mile in twenty minutes, the 61-foot craft was pulled by a single horse which walked the towing path. The horse was hitched to a tow rope sixty feet long, the forerunner of miles of ropes to be used in canal boating days.

Farther west on the frontier, the keelboats of the Missouri

River were towed by rope and men who walked ashore. The rope, sometimes a thousand feet long, was attached to a pulley atop a 30-foot mast and fastened to the bow. A crew of from twenty to forty men, walking Indian-fashion along the bank, would pull the boat while the pilot directed them from the deck. He used a pole to keep the craft from running aground against the shore. This was called cordelling and was the way the keelboats got upstream.

Sometimes, if the river bank would permit it, horses were used. They might be hitched to a rope warped around a tree to pull the boat forward. By men or by horses, the keelboats were towed fifteen miles or more a day against the swift-flowing current.

The sound of a horn at daybreak would call the crew to work and, from then until dark, they would toil half-bent over rocks and through the brush and brambles, in sun, rain or storm. Day

after day, for six months or more, they labored up-river. Coming back down, they could put away the rope and take their ease as they floated with the stream.

Rope was a vital tool of the picturesque Mississippi River steamboats, the first of which came puffing down the river in 1811, just eight years after Napoleon sold the United States the lands of the Louisiana Purchase from which were carved all or part of thirteen later states. Within thirty years, the romantic steamboating days were at their peak, as the gay paddle-wheelers served the rush of new frontier settlement.

Plying the often shallow and shoal-filled waters, the old steamboat pilots depended on rope, not only for normal ship uses, but also to pull free of treacherous sandbars. If there was a tree on the bank near the sandbar where the boat was stuck, a rope would be made fast to it. The other end would be fastened around the boat's capstan, the windlass that would slowly draw the line in as the engine bells jingled to the bucking that shivered her timbers.

Where there were no trees close by for the warping of lines, the pilot would order, "Plant a deadman!" The "deadman" was a log, planted three or four feet deep in a hole dug in the sandbar itself, or in the tree-barren stretch of shore. A rope attached to the middle of the deeply buried log would be used to draw the boat free, sometimes by pulling it right over the sandbar, with a mighty scraping of the bottom, to the clear water on the other side.

On smaller streams and rivers, there were rope ferries, when there were no bridges for coaches and wagons. The small ones were no more than shallow scows, operated by a rope stretched overhead from shore to shore, within grasp of the ferryman who pulled his boat across by hauling hand over hand. In other places, mechanical leverage was used, or a team of horses, to pull the boat across the stream by rope from the far shore.

Ropes hitched to horses pulled the first cars of the pioneer Columbia Railroad between Philadelphia and Pittsburgh, a trip that took four days or more in 1834 by what was called "The Fast Line." But rope played an even more important part than that in the most unusual journey.

The earliest of the horse-drawn railroad cars used on the line looked like stagecoaches of the same period. They were mounted on small flanged wheels, designed to run on the iron-topped wooden rails which were the tracks. When the traveler had been conveyed about two miles outside Philadelphia, a considerable hill interrupted the railroad's progress. The trains, then called "brigades of cars," got over the hill by being pulled up the slope by means of a rope and a stationary steam engine that wound it in from the top of the mountain.

A rope hawser that measured about six inches around was tried at first, but wasn't big enough to do a good job mountain-hauling the cars. It was replaced, after a year's trial, by a nine-inch rope laid at a cost of nearly three thousand dollars. But that was only about one-fourth as much as the total that the railroad finally paid out, during a six-year period, for various hill-pulling hawsers.

When the traveler reached the top of this hill near Philadelphia, he continued on his journey almost to the town of Columbia on the Susquehanna River, where rope again was used to pull the cars up a second hill in the same way. This time, the steam engine at the top drew the rope-hitched cars up a 1,800-foot inclined plane. The traveler then took a packet-boat and set forth on a 172-mile voyage over the central division of the Penn Canal to the terminus at the little town of Hollidaysburg, passing through 108 locks on his way.

At Hollidaysburg, he faced the most unique part of his trip, the thirty-six miles between that town on the east and Johnstown on the west. The two settlements were separated by a crest of the Allegheny Mountains that towered almost 2,300 feet high. It had long been realized that lifting canal boats over such an obstacle by means of locks would cost too much even if engineers could do it. Therefore, it was decided that the route should be carried over the mountains by a rope railroad, the likes of which had never before been seen.

The track-laying crews built a series of step-like inclined planes to lift the traveler's car about a thousand feet in gradual stages over the first ten miles and then lower it more than 1,700 feet, slope by slope, over the twenty-six miles between the highest point and Johnstown on the west. But before the track could be laid, it was necessary to cut a 30-mile path through dense forest. Then two stationary engines, one for reserve use in case of a breakdown, were installed at the top of each inclined plane.

By means of endless ropes, the cars were pulled up the inclines from Hollidaysburg to the summit of the range and lowered down the slope to Johnstown to speed the "Fast Line" passenger on his way toward Pittsburgh. Charles Dickens made the trip during his first visit to the United States in 1842 and described the journey vividly in his *American Notes*.

"On Sunday morning, we arrived at the foot of the mountain which is crossed by railroad," the English author wrote. "There are ten inclined planes, five ascending and five descending; the carriages are dragged up the former, and let slowly down the latter by means of stationary engines; the comparatively level space between being traversed sometimes by horse and sometimes by engine power, as the case demands."

Dickens wrote that the trip was not to be "dreaded for its dangers" because it was very carefully managed, with only two cars traveling at a time, and full safety precautions were taken. But he added that some of the tracks were at the extreme edge of a giddy precipice and that "looking from the carriage window the traveller gazed sheer down, without a stone or scrap of fence between, into the mountain depths below."

Rope soon helped in a still more remarkable scheme put into operation on this rugged railroad. So that the traveler wouldn't have to make so many uncomfortable shiftings from one vehicle to another during his Pittsburgh journey, passenger canal boats were built that could be taken apart in sections and rope-lifted aboard railroad cars made for carrying them over the mountains.

The passenger arriving at Hollidaysburg didn't have to get off the canal packet. He stayed aboard while the whole section was lifted to wheels, rope-hauled up the mountain and lowered down the other side, to be slid again into the water at Johnstown on a reassembled canal boat that carried him along the artificial river toward Pittsburgh.

One of the men working on the project at the time for the state engineering department was a young farmer who had just become a naturalized citizen. Back in his native Germany, he had studied civil engineering and managed to get a degree from a Berlin university. But his dreams had been of freedom from European tyranny and of the great opportunity that America had to offer a young man with the ambition to make his way in the world.

His name was John A. Roebling. With his brother, Karl, he organized a small group of the younger people of his neighborhood and undertook to lead their emigration to the United States. They established a farm colony at Saxonburg, Pennsylvania, and John worked at farming with the others for four years. He landed a job in 1837 with the state canal system and was assigned to the mountain-hauling project between Hollidaysburg and Johnstown.

For him, it was a job filled with troubles, but also the opportunity that brought him success. His troubles came from the bulky ropes of Kentucky hemp that were used to tow the cradle-like cars up the tracks over the cresting Alleghenies. The thick hawsers were hard to handle and, as strong as they were, constantly had to be replaced because of rough usage.

Young John Roebling decided that some substitute for the hemp was needed. For three years, he experimented on his own at his farm at Saxonburg. Rope had been made of wire as far back as the time of the Romans. Fragments of thin copper wire rope were found in the ruins of the volcano-destroyed town of ancient Pompeii. But wire rope had never been used commercially in the United States until Roebling decided to try his hand at making it.

He set up a simple ropewalk in a meadow behind his home and, with the help of some of his farm neighbors, began to hand-lay rope made of iron wire strands. Roebling soon convinced the canal engineers of its value and his wire rope was put into use drawing the cars up the mountain. Word of it quickly spread and he went into the full-time business of making wire rope, still using the meadowland production yard until the demand was great enough for him to establish a factory at Trenton, New Jersey, in 1848.

Roebling adapted the use of his wire rope to the principle of

the suspension bridge in building an aqueduct across the Allegheny River. He went on to become America's celebrated bridge-builder, constructing what were then spectacular engineering wonders of the world.

He spanned the whirling gorge of the Niagara River in 1855 with the first successful railway suspension bridge ever built, bridged the wide Ohio River at Cincinnati, and planned the famous Brooklyn Bridge. But an accident, while working on that, took his life.

Standing atop some wooden pilings of a harbor ferry slip on a summer day in 1869, Roebling was inspecting the site for the location of the bridge's Brooklyn tower when a boat pushed against the poles unexpectedly and crushed his foot, causing a tetanus infection. He died before seeing the first stone laid in the structure that was to crown his career, but the Brooklyn Bridge was carried to completion by his son, Washington Roebling.

Wire rope, in addition to all the other uses it was put to, helped indirectly to change the skyline of New York and other big cities by making possible safe passenger elevators in buildings, and thus the towering skyscrapers themselves, in which people could be lifted to offices stories high.

Before the time of elevators, or "vertical railways" as they were first called, buildings were seldom of more than five stories. Rope-hoisted platforms were used for freight in some of them, but if there were to be taller buildings to put as many offices as possible on small plots of crowded city land, there had to be some kind of "rapid and easy vertical transit" for passengers.

Hoisting machines operated by ropes and pulleys were at least as old as the ancient Greek physicist and inventor, Archimedes, who developed a large rope-winding drum in 236 B.C., which was powered by men walking inside it. Steam hoists of one kind or another were in use in America almost as soon as the steam engine became practical. There were platform elevators in New York in the 1850's and, at about the same time, a Boston firm put sixteen freight elevators, drawn by hempen ropes, into a block of warehouses.

But there were constant accidents due to the breaking of ropes. When Boston inventor Otis Tufts installed the first steam-operated passenger elevator in the old Fifth Avenue Hotel in New York in 1859, people were so amazed that a "vertical railway" was possible, they came in daily crowds, out of curiosity, just to see for themselves that it would really work. That one operated on a large screw on a twenty-inch solid iron shaft, governed by a rope which passed through the car.

Tufts also improved the old rope elevators by having, instead of one single rope to lift them, a number of ropes on which the strain was equally distributed by a system of levers. Almost all elevators soon had two or more ropes yoked to the car, but there were still falls and crashes, and the hardy stair-climbers avoided elevators as an "effeminate and unnecessary innovation," as one editorial writer of the period complained, declaring that it was "unhealthful and unnatural" to use them.

Six wire ropes, each tested to a ten-ton strain, suspended the car placed in the American House in Boston in 1868 and a brass name plate was fixed to it to proclaim proudly that this was a "vertical railway," in case anyone might be in doubt. The intervention of the Civil War, when ropes, wire and other materials were needed for military use, held back the development of elevators, so that it wasn't until around 1870 that they came into wide general use.

By 1840, the number of fiber ropemaking plants in the United States had been reduced to about fifty and the hard times of two depressions in the years before the Civil War forced twenty more companies out of business or consolidated them with larger ones. The remaining rope factories, however, were bigger and working more busily than ever. The clipper ships, steamboats and railroads had more than doubled the value of their output. And, from California, came the cry, "Gold!"

The dramatic discovery at John Sutter's sawmill in 1848 turned the eyes of the nation and most of the world toward the new American West, already being settled by the covered wagon pioneers and the steady migration of people across the Mississippi to new lands. Now, the westward movement became a stampede as "gold fever" drove hundreds of men in the east to quit their homes and jobs and go adventuring with the Forty-niners.

With them, as with the earlier covered wagons, went rope. And not far off were the grass empire years of the cattle ranches and the cowboy, who wouldn't have existed except for rope; the wagon freighters and homesteaders, all needing rope for a tool. Rope haltered the horses of the westward pioneer and hitched teams of mules, made the springs for beds, served in the digging of water wells and the lifting of ore buckets from crude mines, for lariat and as the noose of the law.

At the bookkeeper's desk of a general merchandise firm in Boston, when all New England was in the throes of gold rush excitement, was a young man in his twenties who was as adventurous as most fellows his age, but who had more caution than some.

He was Alfred Tubbs, a New Hampshire lad with quite a bit of commercial experience behind him before he went to work in Boston, and he also thought there was money to be made in California, but not with the miner's pick and shovel. The opportunity he saw was in the rope and other merchandise the booming new West would need. His employers sent him to San Francisco in 1850, at the age of 22, to test the new market.

Alfred sailed from New York, crossed the Panama Isthmus and, in an unusually quick trip, reached San Francisco on a second steamer in about six weeks. He sold his goods, took a look around, and decided to stay and go into the rope and ship chandlery business. In a letter he wrote home to his father, he said that although San Francisco was then nothing but a rough and rowdy village, he felt it was destined to become "a great rich metropolis, the capital of a new American Empire commanding the trade of the Orient, Australia and the islands of the Pacific."

He served on the Vigilance Committee that tried to bring order to the wild and reckless town of incoming gold seekers and home-going failures and, as his rope sales prospered, he urged his older brother, Hiram, a Boston hotel keeper, to join him. Hiram arrived in 1853 aboard a vessel that ran aground in a dense fog just outside San Francisco Bay.

Fortunately, it struck a sandy beach between two rocky cliffs that would have pounded it apart. Hiram and his wife, along with some 600 other passengers of the steamer *Tennessee,* turned the panic of a threatened shipwreck into a happy lark. With coffee made over driftwood fires and food from the stranded vessel, they had a picnic on the beach while waiting for mule-drawn buckboards to take them on their way.

Alfred and Hiram Tubbs went into partnership supplying the San Francisco shipping trade with rope and gear. They bought an interest in several ships and outfitted them for whaling. But their main business was rope and they faced the problem of not being able to get enough of it from the eastern ropewalks to fill their orders promptly. Shipments took months to reach the coast. The solution seemed to be in setting up their own rope factory, but they faced no easy task at a time when hardly anything used in San Francisco was manufactured there.

Hiram returned hopefully to Boston to buy the machinery and to assemble a crew of expert ropemakers to come out and set it up and operate the plant. But he found very little machinery for sale. Most of the eastern rope mills made their equipment in their own machine shops and nobody was manufacturing rope-making machines. He had to search all over New England for them and have some made by hand.

Recruiting men for promised jobs in the unknown future of far-off California was even more difficult. Hiram wanted experts who had learned through years of training and experience how to prepare hemp, and twist and lay it into rope, and such men already had secure positions. They were far from eager to tear up roots in communities where they had lived all their lives, to sell their homes and move themselves and their families halfway around the world.

After months of effort, he succeeded in his quest, with the men signed and the machinery ready to send from Boston on several ships. The first lot of rope machines and mechanics who had been hired to help put them together arrived in San Francisco in midwinter. Fourteen ropemakers came back with Hiram Tubbs the next spring.

The brothers had handled rope and sold it and they knew what good qualities finished rope should have, but neither of them had ever made any rope. They had to depend entirely on the New England ropemakers and on learning from their own mistakes by trial and error. There were many delays as the factory was completed and the first test runs were made.

San Francisco was still hardly more than an overgrown mining camp and the state less than half a dozen years old. Nothing so important as rope had been manufactured there. The 1,000-foot ropewalk was the first establishment of its kind outside the long-settled east. It was the cause for cheering community celebration when, in July, 1856, the men who had come from Boston turned out the first commercial rope ever made in the west.

During the Civil War, the United States Navy, which had its own ropewalks that could turn out all the cordage needed for peacetime use, had to call on outside ropemakers for extra supplies. Although naval vessels as well as merchant ships were becoming steam-powered, most of the steamships carried auxiliary sails and also needed rope for other purposes. But at war's end, sales of rope for ships fell off sharply for a time and the ropemakers, in search of new markets, began to develop ropes and twines to meet highly specialized requirements.

The petroleum industry, which was to grow into the biggest single user of rope, already was turning out five times as much oil as at the start of the war and wanted ropes built to do many special jobs for which ordinary rope was unsuitable.

Pennsylvania's oil rush of 1859, ten years after the gold rush in California, was on a smaller scale than the search for gold, but just as colorful and turbulent. The oil prospectors changed our way of life and uncovered far more wealth in the earth than California's gold seekers ever could, even though, at the time, they were merely looking for a substitute for whale oil to light the nation's homes.

Before the Civil War, when there was any need for home lighting at night, it came mostly from the dim tallow candle or glass-chimneyed whale oil lamp. Some folks, especially in rural areas, just went to bed at sundown and seldom used artificial light at all. Candles, of course, needed string for wicks and the whalers used rope in their hunt for whales to produce lamp oil. But they never needed rope in the kinds and quantities that the natural oil industry soon was to demand.

Whale oil was becoming scarcer and more expensive by mid-century, with whales being killed at such a rate that the whalers had to range ever farther out to sea in their hunt for them. Many substitutes were tried, but none proved satisfactory until kerosene oil was produced from coal. Still wanted was a less expensive source for kerosene to light the lamps. Natural petroleum, then called "rock oil," was collected only from seepage in the ground.

A former railroad conductor from upstate New York, Edwin L. Drake, had invested in one of the "rock oil" companies. In 1857, he went to look over the company's property at Oil Creek, near the village of Titusville, Pennsylvania. What he saw confirmed his zealous belief that oil could be drilled from a hole in the ground.

He was employed to conduct the drilling operations. With a courage that refused to admit defeat against the odds of earlier failures, Drake completed the first commercially successful well in 1859 at the depth of sixty-nine feet.

Almost overnight, as soon as the shouted news spread, the

peaceful countryside around Titusville, which became the business center of the new oil fields, was an oozing quagmire where fortune-hunters madly scrambled for quick wealth. They came from all parts of the country, as well as from nearby towns, some of them rough, greedy and brawling.

Wooden derricks sprang up everywhere, flimsy shacks and open vats, and the wasted oil scummed over lakes and streams. Fire, a constant menace, wiped out many fields. Rope drilled the wells and pulled the barges that floated the barreled crude petroleum down Oil Creek. Boom towns sprang up and flourished mightily, some of them to die when oil, dreams and money ran out.

But from the wells of Pennsylvania came the oil industry, which produced only 2,000 barrels of crude oil the year Drake drilled his first well, as compared with the billions of barrels of oil

that now come yearly from more than 500,000 producing wells in twenty-nine states. And the oil men needed tons and tons of rope, not only in the fields, but also for the barges and the whole enormous job of transporting oil by water and land.

For drilling the wells, not just any rope would do. The ropemakers had to produce a dozen kinds of cordage, precision-laid for specific work. Rope was the main implement of the cable tool method of drilling which was used up until the turn of the century. Cable tools still are used in some areas today, especially for shallow holes in soft earth formations, although rotary drilling has become more usual.

Derricks of open framework, now of steel and some as tall as a 20-story building, are used in both methods to support the equipment that must be lowered into the well. In cable tool drilling, a "string" of tools, consisting of a heavy bit and stem on the end of a cable, was connected end to end and alternately raised and dropped so the bit could pound its way into the earth to pulverize the soil and rock.

The string of tools was removed at intervals so water could be flushed into the hole and the resulting "slurry" of drill cuttings removed by bailing them out. As the hole deepened, it might be lined with casing to keep it from caving in. All of this was heavy and exacting work that put the ropes to extremely hard use, straining them with heavy loads at fiber-burning speed against the rubbing friction of dirt, sand and rock. Failure of a rope was a serious matter that could mean the loss of tools as well as time and labor.

Rotary drilling, now used in most American wells, was developed in the 1890's. The rotary method uses an augerlike bit attached to the lower end of a string of connected lengths of steel drill pipe. This is revolved by means of a turntable on the derrick floor.

As it turns, the bit bores a hole, in much the same way as a carpenter's auger bores through wood, and lengths of pipe are added as the hole deepens. A mixture of water, clay and chemicals is pumped down through the drill pipe to the bottom to flush the cuttings from the well and form a cake on the walls of the hole.

Drilling cables had to be of tough manila. Where wire rigs were used, short lengths of special fiber rope called "crackers" were needed for more elasticity and spring. Rotary drills required "cat lines" to hoist pipe and tools. There were big, hard-lay "bull ropes," sometimes three inches thick and more than a hundred feet long, to transmit power from the engine to the grooved pulleys of the "bull wheel," a large reel which wound the cable for drilling or cleaning out the wells.

Ropes used on smaller power wheels were called "calf ropes," and there were "spinning lines" to lower high explosives into the well, and the bluntly-named but vital "belly buster," a safety rope strung across a derrick for a man to lean against as he latched a lifting collar to a drill pipe.

Most of these, and many other special ropes, are still used by the oil industry today, as well as rope for off-shore drilling operations and for the big oil tankers. From the petroleum that rope helped to produce has come rope itself, made of some of the man-created modern synthetic fibers.

But back in the days when the ropemakers were becoming specialists, perhaps the second greatest demand for something more than a run-of-the-mill product was from shops and factories which had turned to steam and needed power transmission ropes. Before there was electricity to drive machines, rope conveyed the power of the steam engines that turned the wheels of American industry. It was fairly inexpensive and any number of endless ropes, belted by splicing or with metal couplings, could be taken off a single drive wheel.

Still used extensively in loading and unloading ships, hard coal mining and many other operations, rope transmission was standard in nearly all factories before 1900. But ordinary rope often frayed and parted in friction against the sheaves and from the strain of bending over pulleys. If it wasn't uniform in weight, diameter and lay, it might jump or slip. Rope failure or replacement meant factory work had to stop.

Power transmission at the coal mines operated jigs and shakers which had to run without interruption to handle the preparation of the raw coal arriving at the headhouse. Stevedores were as much in need of absolute dependability for high speed hoisting. Other users came to the ropemakers with their particular problems.

Rope with a "heart," or inner core, seemed to serve the best. It usually was four strands, or sometimes six, instead of the three strands of standard rope, and had a separate lubricated fiber center to cut down the internal friction. The twist of the threads, lay of the strands and limit of stretch were controlled to suit the exact kind of work to be done. The lubricant usually was tallow and the whole rope had to be carefully blended fiber of the highest grade. Such power transmission rope took truly expert manufacture.

Farmers were becoming more particular, too, in the materials they chose for binding their crops. Western wheat was being reaped by machinery in the late 1800's, but the soft iron wire first used to bind the sheaves brought troubles. Broken bits of it got into the machines and also caused damage at the flour mills.

Ropemakers were soon producing a binder twine, a single yarn twisted to the precise size and strength needed. Automatic hay balers, when they came, also took twine. There were other types made for fish lines, nets and seines, and still different twines for tying various kinds of bundles and packages.

But not all ropes were for work. Some brought entertainment. Theaters before the turn of the century, as much as those of today, depended on ropes to hold scenery and to change it and to pull the curtains so the show could go on. Stagehands used a "lash line" to fasten together flat standing units of scenery. They laced the rope across a series of metal cleats down the rear edges to lash one piece of scenery to the next.

Scenery hung from above was worked by the ropes that came

down from a gridiron high above the stage, called the "fly space," which was a hundred feet or more over the heads of the actors on some big stages. This framework platform had slots running from front to back about every foot or so to accommodate the fly ropes which hung down to the top of the scenery. Above these was a pulley arrangement, over which the ropes ran, as with blocks and tackle.

Half-inch manila ropes were attached to the center and two ends of the hanging piece of scenery, passed over the three blocks above them, and then through a common head block at the side. The ropes were brought down and tied to a row of belaying pins racked along what was called the "pin rail." This was a double set of heavy wooden beams to hold the thirty or more scenery lines that might be needed.

When the particular scene arrived, the "flyman" would loosen the rope from the upper pin and let the slack play through his fingers until the rope became taut on its fastening to the lower pin. He knew that the set had dropped into the right position, since the rope had been measured out beforehand. In that way, he could change his sets quickly and not make the audience wait for a complicated rigging of the scenes.

The fly gallery was eliminated in some theaters and the flying of scenery handled by a system of ropes and sandbags or other counterweights operated directly from the stage floor to block pulleys above. When a rope was released from its ties, the weight attached to it came down and the scenery flew up out of sight. A careful safety-check of the ropes was necessary because scenery as well as sandbags had been known to fall on unwary actors.

Back in those days long before a television set in every home, when an occasional show of any kind was a rare treat, there was no greater thrill for the whole family than the yearly coming of the circus. But, without ropes, there probably would have been no circuses to wander the towns of the dusty back roads or to set up canvas on the city lots.

Rope was as necessary to the men who put up the Big Tops

as it was to sailors. And without daring aerialists on the ropes at the top of the tent, what would any circus performance have been? Rope walking, or "rope dancing" as it was called, was popular even centuries ago in ancient China and Egypt and was a favorite spectacle with the early Romans. Emperor Marcus Aurelius passed a law to protect rope dancers with safety nets.

There were wandering rope dancers in Europe in medieval times and during the celebration in Paris in 1385 of the marriage of French King Charles VI to Isabel of Bavaria, a performer with two burning candles in his hands walked a rope tied over the roof tops from a bridge to a church steeple. An even more daring fellow performed at the coronation of Edward VI in 16th-century England by sliding down a slanted rope on his head.

An aerialist who called himself The Wingless Birdman thrilled English street crowds of the same period by coasting down a rope on a board thrown on it like a sled. It must have been a spectacular performance indeed, according to contemporary accounts, because during the six-second flight down 150 yards of rope on his stomach, he managed to fire a pistol, blow a trumpet, and leave a trail of smoke behind him.

The Wingless Birdman had an imitator who tried to improve the act by sending a donkey flying down a rope. He made the donkey a metal chest protector and weighted its feet. But the rope broke and the donkey fell on the crowd, bowling people over in a great confusion that resulted in some minor injuries. The donkey, it is said, escaped unhurt because the people beneath broke its fall. No lives were lost, but the rope pulled down part of the church steeple to which it was hitched and the performer, presumably astride his flying donkey, quickly beat it out of town.

A favorite performer of Napoleon was a woman tightrope walker known as Madame Saqui. She put on her act at night, suddenly appearing high on the rope in the darkness amid a burst of fireworks.

The tightrope walker, who usually performed on a high rope, had to center himself directly over it and often used a balancing pole to help lower the center of gravity. On a low rope, closer to the ground and with more slack to it, the rope dancer sometimes used a parasol so the pressure of air on its surface would help keep him steady. He did faster and more intricate steps, swinging back and forth, pretending falls, and other thrilling tricks.

Perhaps the most famous of all aerialists was the celebrated Emile Blondin, who did all sorts of spectacular stunts on a rope high above Niagara Falls. His real name was Jean François Gravelet and he was born at St. Omer, France, in 1824. When he was only five years old, he was sent to a school for gymnasts at Lyons to be trained as an acrobat and he made his first public appearance there, as The Little Wonder, less than a year later.

Blondin performed for more than sixty-five years, but he was in his thirties before he gained world-wide recognition. He walked a rope across the River Seine near Paris and the Thames in England and began the first of his American appearances in New

York in the 1850's. His name was soon in the newspaper head-lines, where he managed to keep it most of his life with one dar-ing sensation after another.

His first of many crossings of Niagara Falls, on a tight rope 1,100 feet long, was in June, 1859. Blindfolded, he walked the slippery rope, drenched with the spray of the cataract, 160 feet above the rocks and the roaring water. The feat was acclaimed around the world, as well as by the crowd that watched with held breath and then gave out a mighty cheer as Blondin reached the other side.

But that was only the start of Blondin's stunts on the rope above the falls. He made other crossings with a sack tied over him, walking on stilts, and trundling a wheelbarrow. He balanced himself on chairs suspended over the splashing falls and even carried a cookstove out to the center of the rope, squatted down

there and cooked and ate an omelet. He took adventurous passengers across, carrying them on his back, for twenty-five dollars a trip.

It amused him to invite famous people to take the ride. A story he often repeated was about England's future King Edward VII, then the Prince of Wales, eldest son of Queen Victoria. The Prince apparently was strongly tempted to accept the invitation to ride pick-a-back across the falls, but reluctantly had to refuse.

When one of the other passengers he was carrying on the rope nervously began squirming around, Blondin stopped the dangerous shifting about on his shoulders by warning, "Sir, I must request you to sit still or I will have to put you down right here."

How much he earned from his Niagara Falls rope walking is not known, but the tremendous publicity sent Blondin back to England as one of the biggest box-office attractions of the century and he was soon on his way to making a comfortable fortune. He appeared at London's Crystal Palace in 1861, turning somersaults on a rope stretched across the central hall 170 feet above the ground.

For some thirty more years, he went on performing other feats high up on his rope. In 1875, passengers aboard a ship on which he was traveling swooned and fainted when he staged an exhibition. Blondin skipped back and forth across a 450-foot rope stretched between two masts while the ship was steaming along at thirteen knots and rolling heavily.

After he went into semi-retirement, he still attracted newspaper publicity, probably deliberately, by the daily strolls he took in the garden of his estate. Instead of keeping to the walks among the flowers, Blondin strolled along a rope high above the garden. His last public performance was in Belfast in 1896, a year before his death in London at the age of seventy-three.

Meanwhile, the ropemakers were turning more to machinery, sometimes still reluctantly, to replace the lingering hand operations of their ropewalks. Although machines already were being used by some in forming the strands and laying them into rope, the preparing of the fiber and spinning of it into yarn, first steps in the process, were largely done by hand.

Inventor John Good helped bring the change to complete machine manufacture of rope. Born in County Roscommon, Ireland, near where the River Shannon flows, Good was left fatherless at an early age and his mother, after struggling along for a few years, hopefully emigrated with the boy to the United States and settled in Brooklyn, New York. Young John went to a parochial school for a time, but at the age of twelve started work in the ropewalk of Henry Lawrence and Sons.

He worked there four years, gaining a thorough knowledge of hand ropemaking. When he was sixteen, he decided also to learn the machinist's trade and apprenticed himself to James Bulgar's machine shop for four years. Good then returned to the ropewalk in 1861, at the age of twenty, to become its young foreman. All the operations at that ropewalk then were still being done by hand.

Good began to apply his machinist's knowledge and experience to devising ropemaking machinery. He experimented at home and in his spare time for nearly eight years before receiving his first patent for a machine called a "breaker," designed to draw the fibers into the tiny threads known as "slivers" that are spun into the basic yarn of rope. Although it was a great labor-saving device, Good was unable to talk any rope manufacturer into buying the rights to his machine.

He set up a machine shop of his own in 1870 to make the breakers himself. Good finally did manage to sell some of the rights to manufacture it to an English concern that introduced the breaker to the British Isles. Within a few years, his breaker had replaced the old hand operation in most of the hard-fiber rope plants throughout the world. He continued to make the breakers in the United States and to patent and manufacture other ropemaking machines that built his little Brooklyn shop into a big business.

Good was granted a patent in 1873 for a "nipper" for a spinning jenny, which meant that for the first time, by means of rollers, rope yarn could be spun without cutting. Two years later, he devised a regulator for his fiber-drawing and spinning machine. Next was what was called a "measuring stop motion." From Good's creative mind came a whole flood of ropemaking inventions which he patented to modify his breakers, nippers, spreaders and regulators.

He confined his attention entirely to making machinery for fifteen years. But in 1885, Good decided to go into the making of rope on a large scale himself. He built a big plant at Ravenswood, Long Island, preparing to carry out his plans, and erected two other overseas plants on manufacturing sites he bought near London. Good hoped to capture a major part of the whole world's rope business by using his factories to make what he called a "new process" rope, based on one of the patents he had obtained.

This method, according to Good, would make rope so much stronger than any then being made that lower quality and cheaper grades of fiber could be used and still give a product of ample strength for any need. Rope could be produced in all sizes of hemp, sisal or jute at prices slashed so low that other manufacturers would be unable to meet them.

Such were Good's plans of conquering the rope market. And his reputation as an inventor was such that the threat must have been considered a real one by a group of other manufacturers who had organized a trust of their own to try to control the production and sale of rope in the United States. They attempted to corner supplies of raw fiber, set up a monopoly of manufacture, and fix their own prices.

With a starting capital of a million and a half dollars, the combine bought up a number of smaller mills and invited others to join. Several companies, among them the largest that are still operating today, held out. But at one period, the group controlled eighty per cent of the nation's rope output and boosted the value of its stock to fifteen million dollars. It was one of the first of the country's big industrial trusts, before the days of stricter Federal regulation.

Before Good's factories were ready to go into actual production, he was asked to join the big combine. He refused, but he never opened the plants he had built to make his cheap "new process" rope. Instead, in 1888, he accepted an offer of $150,000 a year from the group *not* to make rope. He agreed to keep his plants closed and stay out of competition.

Three years later, he signed a contract to manufacture his machinery exclusively for the rope trust. When the contract was cancelled in 1892, Good plunged into the ropemaking business as an aggressive competitor. But by that time, the big combine itself was on the verge of bankruptcy that shook the financial world.

Good's ropemaking concern lasted until 1897, when the general hard times of the depression, that ended only after the Spanish-American War, put him out of business. He died in 1908 at the age of sixty-seven, after two other attempts to set up rope companies failed.

But, throughout his entire lifetime, Good not only managed his various manufacturing concerns, but also continued his experimental work. His inventions in ropemaking machinery involved more than one hundred patents and are the basis of much of the equipment used to make rope today in three-fourths of the world's hard-fiber rope factories.

Cotton rope also came into many new uses during the 1800's because of a series of inventions that led to improved methods of braiding it. Strictly speaking, the rope that most of us know best, the common backyard cotton clothesline, isn't rope at all. It is cotton cord and technically doesn't become braided rope until it gets into its larger sizes.

While to most people rope is anything made of several strands, whether twisted or braided, it properly should be called "cord" or "line" until it gets up to about an inch or more in diameter. Sailors call cordage of less than one inch "small stuff."

There were cotton ropes in very ancient times and cotton was cultivated in America in the Jamestown colony in 1607. Probably the first braiding machine ever built was invented by Thomas Walford of Manchester, England, in 1748. The braiding of cotton cord spread to France and then to Germany, where the Barmen district became the center of the industry that supplied the world, with a later business that grew until 100,000 machines were used there.

But in the United States, it wasn't until after Eli Whitney's cotton gin greatly increased production of the soft fiber in 1794 that braided cotton gradually became the standard household "rope" of so many uses. Among the early American manufacturers of cotton braids was William Horstmann of Philadelphia. He brought machines from Germany in the early 1800's to make cordage to cover the wire supports of the hoop skirts women wore at the time.

The ladies of fashion demanded more cord for their hoop skirts than Horstmann could make and, unable to get additional braiding machines from Germany, he asked a Rhode Island concern to make them. The result was a braiding machine that became the foundation of a soon-flourishing American industry. Philadelphia was the first center of the trade, but before long, Rhode Island took over. A Providence man, listed in old records only as Mr. J. Thorp, was granted the first American patent for a braiding machine in 1821, but there were some thirty others invented during the next half-century.

While hoop skirts created the necessity that led to the early development of braided cotton cordage, the braiding method in general use took its name from the Maypole dancers of medieval times who held streamers attached to the top of a Maypole and criss-crossed in and out to weave them as they danced around the pole. The machine-made cotton cord was "Maypole braided," plaited so that the strands of spun cotton yarn ran diagonally around the cord.

As more modern methods were developed, this process became the "hollow braiding" that is used to make a great part of today's cotton cordage. Despite the term "hollow," the cord often contains a fairly large center strand of cotton, jute or sometimes strong nylon core.

Hollow braided cord has great freedom from stretch and twist. The center sometimes is of loosely roven material, easily pulled apart by itself, but it acts as a soft inner cushion for the braids. Less expensive cords may be made entirely of this roving, formed into large strands that can be braided, instead of separate threads of yarn.

Windows in all homes and other buildings, before today's casements and picture windows, usually were the familiar double-hung sliding type. The sash was balanced with cast iron or lead weights attached to sash cords that ran over pulleys and millions of feet of cotton cords were used for these.

It was to the problem of finding a better sash cord, one that was rounder, firmer and less likely to break under the constant pulley friction of opening and closing windows, that New England cordage maker James P. Tolman applied himself in the 1880's. Tolman was working at the time for a cordage firm near Boston. In his spare hours, he developed a machine that would produce what later became known as a "solid braid."

The many small strands of cotton yarn were braided in such a way that they ran almost lengthwise of the cord instead of around it. Strain and wear were distributed equally over all the little strands rather than only on the outside. The result was a smooth, non-kinking cord, easy to tie, not as likely to ravel, and ready to last for up to fifty years of use in the average window.

Tolman offered his machine to the company that employed

him but, perhaps because the invention came at a time when business generally was in a financial panic, the company refused it. Convinced of the value of his invention, he started in business for himself in 1884 with a small factory at Boston's Fort Hill Square to make his solid braided cord.

Four years later, the demand was so great Tolman opened a bigger factory at Shirley, Massachusetts. The cord he designed for window sashes soon was being used for a hundred other things, from cowboy lariats to the city street lamps that then had to be rope-lowered for lighting, for dog sled lines and to guide the power rods of the nation's clanging trolley cars.

The first of the automobiles wasn't far off, opening another market to makers of all kinds of rope. Early motorists carried rope as a standard tool aboard the gas buggies that chugged over poor roads likely to toss a begoggled and duster-clad adventurer into a ditch or hub-deep mudhole. Rope hitched to a tree or towed by a farmer's horse pulled him out of his trouble more frequently than did the sputtering engine under the hood.

Rope also pulled the air gliders that led to the early experiments of two men who tossed a coin as they stood on a cold and windy North Carolina beach in December, 1903, deciding who should be the first to try the flying machine they had made. For many years, in many places, man had tried to hitch rope to wings, as these two had with their gliders. But the ropes and gliders finally had been put aside that day, because there was an engine in the machine to give it power of its own.

The man who had called the flip of the coin, shivering in his dark gray business suit, lay flat on his stomach between the wings as the motor roared and lurched the flimsy contraption over a crude runway to lift it ten feet in the air. Nobody had come out from town to watch and there really wasn't much to see. The flying machine stayed up about twelve seconds and then flopped back to earth after going only 120 feet.

At the controls, of course, was Orville Wright, who won the coin toss from his brother, Wilbur, and thus became the first man

to fly without need of rope to pull a glider. Such was the birth of aviation that would use more tons of more kinds of specialized rope than any ropemaker could then dream. Rope would be needed for lashing planes down, for fueling them in the sky, for towing and for targets, and to make the nets that would catch them to a stop on someday-to-come aircraft carriers.

During the same period, construction of the great Panama Canal finally got underway and one American ropemaking company alone received the largest single order in its history, a call for one million pounds of rope to help build it. Without rope, the work would have been impossible and, before it was finished in 1914, that amount looked comparatively small.

By then, a Serbian nationalist at Sarajevo had assassinated Archduke Francis Ferdinand, heir to the throne of Austria-Hungary, and set off the powder keg of European rivalries that brought the First World War. Manila fiber rose sharply in price and the better grades became scarce, which led ropemakers to a greater use of other fibers from cactus-like plants such as henequen.

Most henequen came from Mexico's flat and humid Yucatan Province and the Mexican government set up a monopoly to fix prices. Henequen and other types of sisal were planted extensively in Caribbean countries, East Africa and the Dutch East Indies to break the monopoly. They soon captured much of the trade and sisal became second only to manila as a fiber for ropemaking.

But it was the Second World War that brought the United States the most crucial need for rope in its history. Among Japan's first targets of war, after Pearl Harbor, was the island of Mindanao in the Philippines, source of manila fiber for the rope America needed to win a war. Only a few hours after Hawaii was hit on December 7, 1941, dive-bombers from other Japanese carriers attacked an American warship in Davao Gulf in the Philippines.

Within three weeks, the Japanese landed an amphibious force on Mindanao, seized thousands of bales of fiber and shut off shipments for the rest of the war. Soon they moved against other fiber outlets in the Pacific, to control the ports of the East Indies as well as the Philippines, cutting off the flow of sisal in addition to manila. The actions cost the United States most of its normal peacetime supply of raw materials for making rope.

Long before the actual outbreak of war, rope had been put on the first lists of critical materials, along with rubber and tin. By stockpiling supplies, America managed to have enough on hand to meet its first immediate war needs. The amount was small, however, against the wartime demands that soon overwhelmed the ropemakers. America at war required four times as much rope as during peacetime and had little to make it with.

The army wanted rope for tents, tarpaulins, drag lines and for all the uses of trucks, tanks, guns, bridges and airplanes. The navy needed far more rope than its ships had ever used in the great days under sail, rope for mooring, lines for refueling, for lifeboats and for towing. Aircraft carriers consumed miles of rope and the mobile service units that kept the carriers at sea needed rope to deliver food, bombs, shells, spare parts and even to replace men with new personnel put aboard the vessels.

In addition, there was the merchant marine, the farmers producing the nation's food, all the thousands of industries making things to support the war effort. Hardly any raw material was coming in and there were almost no sources of ropemaking fiber that had been developed at home. Obviously, new sources were needed urgently, and the government encouraged any plan that seemed likely to produce the materials for rope.

The Department of Agriculture distributed seeds and offered farmers a subsidy to grow American hemp, too costly to produce in commercial quantity during peacetime. Imports of sisal from Mexico, Cuba and Haiti were boosted. Jute, raffia, coir fiber from the husk of coconuts and many unusual mixtures and blends, as well as fibers the rope industry previously had discarded, were used to stretch supplies.

As early as 1925, the Agriculture Department had been interested in experimental planting of abaca, the manila fiber plant, in Central America. Root stocks of six of the best commercial varieties were brought to Panama from the Philippines and the United Fruit Company agreed to cooperate by making experimental plantings on its lands. The company carried on research for five years on a 50-acre plot that was developed.

When war clouds gathered in the late 1930's, the government encouraged the company to expand its holdings to two thousand acres. The Japanese attack on Pearl Harbor brought an agreement to boost the plantings to an eventual 28,000 acres in Honduras, Guatemala, Costa Rica and Panama. The government was given free use of the company's land and the fiber, used mainly for marine cordage, was produced without profit to serve war needs.

At the end of the war, production was maintained on a management fee basis until the government decided there was no need for it to continue in the abaca business in Central America. The projects gradually were shut down during the 1950's so that very little, if any, abaca was being produced in the Western Hemisphere. But during the war and in the years right after it, the plantings went far to help meet the critical rope shortage.

Before the war, ninety-five per cent of abaca fiber came from the Philippines and the rest from the East Indies. It was mostly the early Japanese settlers in the Philippine province of Davao who had started the industry and who lived and prospered on it until the invading forces from Japan all but destroyed it. Wartime occupation, guerrilla actions and political unrest when peace finally came, held back the work of restoring production both in the Philippines and in the Indies. Shortages of manila rope continued in peacetime until the great Philippine plantations slowly were rebuilt.

Out of all the substitutes tried during the war came one group of materials that found a permanent place in ropemaking, the man-made synthetic fibers. There had been experiments with nylon before the war, but it was considered mostly a novelty, in short supply and high in price for widespread commercial use.

Wartime needs for rope of great strength and stretch for special requirements, such as towing troop-laden gliders behind airplanes, found an answer in nylon. Tested under fire in many ways, it soon was made in quantities that improved commercial production and reduced costs. By war's end, its general use was accepted and other synthetic fibers for making rope were on the way.

Although natural fiber ropes still do most of the jobs for which rope is needed, synthetic ropes are replacing them rapidly in many fields of work and sport. Some ropemakers are convinced that our standard rope of the future may be of these man-made materials and that someday natural fiber ropes may be as much a curiosity of the past as the cordage that was hand-twisted in the old ropewalks.

Whether that happens or not, synthetics already have made possible the use of smaller and lighter ropes with a strength equal to larger ropes of natural fiber, thus opening new markets for braided as well as twisted cord. But whatever the materials of rope, the basic idea behind the making of it hasn't changed since ancient man first twisted together the tendrils of wild wines.

Modern ropemaking is a specialized process that uses constant research and the highly-developed techniques of science to produce what amount to precision tools, ropes manufactured with great skill and care to meet exact needs. Machines that now take only a fraction of the space of the ropewalks turn out far better rope than that made crudely and slowly by hand.

But the main difference is in the process, not in the age-old method by which threads become yarn and yarn forms strands through the various opposite twistings that finally are laid into rope. The necessity that makes rope part of everything we take for granted in our daily lives remains unchanged, as it has through all the centuries of man.

With rope, we have made our civilization and our world and, whatever tomorrow's world, we probably will need rope to help build it.

Old English Rope Walk

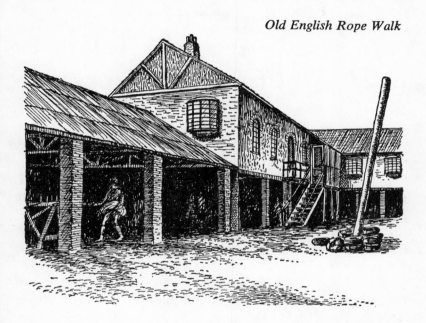

2

How to Choose and Use Rope

Rope serves as a tool for many different purposes, but obviously no one rope will do all of them equally well.

The wrong rope may mean spoiled fun, ruined work, damage to property or even an accident in which someone is hurt. But use of the right kind of rope can make dozens of jobs easier, add to the skill of sports, the enjoyment of camping and boating, and help in hundreds of day-to-day chores from the tying of boxes to the towing of stalled cars.

Choosing rope to get the best use and most fun from it doesn't require expert knowledge, but it probably will help in selecting it to understand something a little more about the materials that go into it and the ways in which it is made.

Rope fibers vary greatly in strength, in resisting wear and rot, in smoothness of handling and in other important qualities.

Manila makes the best and strongest natural hard-fiber rope. Good manila rope, when new, is hard and pliant and yellowish in color. While it is somewhat hairy looking, like all new rope, it is far smoother than others and the fibers feel almost silky when drawn through the hand. More properly called abaca, manila has a strength about the same as an equal cross-section of mild steel.

The fiber comes from a type of banana plant which flourishes to a height three times that of a man in the river valley soil and tropical climate of the Philippines. Cultivated from a shoot, the average plant takes about two years to bear its small and seedy fruit, which is when the plant is cut down to harvest the fiber. Natives split the giant green stalks and peel away layers. These are scraped by hand under saw-toothed knife blades, or by machine, after being piled high on the backs of mules to carry them to where the work is done.

Strong men are needed to heft the thirty-five-pound sections of stalk into the machines or to pull them by hand under the blades that strip them of unwanted pulp. They get about two pounds of fiber from one hundred pounds of stalk. The job must be done quickly once the stalks are cut because they discolor rapidly. Great care must be used to avoid bruising them. When the fiber has been stripped, hanks of it are hung to dry in the sun, just as clothes might be put out on the line, but in fields that cover many acres.

The dry fiber is rolled into bundles called "bultos" and taken to the warehouses by trucks or boats. In the warehouses, the fiber is cleaned and the tips are cut. Native Filipino experts who have spent their entire lives at the task work with laboratory technicians to grade and classify the abaca according to color, length and strength of fiber, and how clean it is.

Scales weigh out the proper amounts for 275-pound bales and box men prepare it for pressing, often by climbing atop the bins to squeeze it down with their feet. The bales are then cart-hauled to the docks to be put aboard lighters and transferred to ships that will bring the fiber to American ropemakers. There are more than twenty grades of abaca, but the lightest in color and the strongest go into "best quality" manila rope.

Sisal is the other hard fiber common to present-day rope-making. Although it doesn't have some of the superior qualities of manila, it is the most widely-used substitute for less expensive rope and also for baler and binder twines. Sisal serves many jobs well when stronger and more durable manila is not required.

It is about three-fourths as strong as manila, which means that larger sizes often have to be used for the same work if it is chosen in place of manila. Sisal generally is not recommended for heavy hoisting. Nearly white in color, sometimes with a tinge of yellow-green, it is not so glossy as manila. The fibers are stiff and brittle, not so silky to the touch, and they tend to splinter.

But when chosen to do a job proper for it, sisal rope sometimes resists abrasion even better than manila. The quality depends a great deal on where the fiber comes from. Usually it takes its name from its place of growth. There is East African Sisal, Brazilian Sisal, Madagascar Sisal and many other kinds. Java Sisal, which comes from the East Indies, is considered the finest.

Sisalana fiber is produced from the sword-like leaves of an Agave cactus plant, kin to the Century Plant, that looks something like a giant pineapple with spikes four feet long. It takes up to five years from the time plants are set out in rows of suckers from the roots of old plants until they grow to the point of harvest. Crops are then cut once or twice a year, for as long as six years afterwards, until the plant finally blossoms and dies.

The cutting is done by hand, but stripping machines called "decorticators" separate the pulp from the fiber and wash the fiber clean by means of a series of sprays and knives that scrape along the length of the leaves. It is then dried and brushed to be classified and put into bales. Sometimes sisal is used in mixtures with manila, as well as by itself, for making rope and twine.

Mexico is the oldest sisal producing country, but today's ropemakers classify the fiber from Mexico's henequen plant separately from other sisals. Henequen, native to Yucatan, often is called "Mexican Sisal," but is used chiefly for lower grades of cordage. It is harsh, coarse and has less strength and durability.

Hemp, which is a soft or "bast" fiber, seldom is used in modern commercial ropemaking. Until a generation or two ago, it was the most popular of all the fibers, but better materials and the high labor costs of producing it have pushed hemp out of the market.

Because it once was so widely used, people got into the habit of calling many kinds of rope "hemp." Since true hemp, which has the formal name *Cannabis sativa,* is a particular plant, it is incorrect to refer to such things as "manila hemp" or "cotton hemp," as people sometimes do. Its main use today is for very high grade twines and for small tarred marine cordage.

Jute is the most extensively used of all soft vegetable fibers except cotton. Like hemp, it is a bast fiber, but although it is soft and has less strength and wearing quality than manila or sisal, it often serves well as a substitute for harder rope and makes some of the most popular twines for industrial tying.

However, its greatest use is for making oakum, linoleum, burlap and other sacking material such as webbing for upholstery. It is one of the most useful and versatile fibers known to industry. Most of the jute that comes to American ropemakers is from Pakistan and India. The stems rather than the leaves are used for fiber in a process that is centuries old.

During February, when the rivers are low, cultivation begins in the lowlands along the banks near the water's edge. Then, a few months later, the midlands are sown. When the water rises still more, usually in May, jute is planted in the uplands.

Crude wooden plows drawn by cattle blade open the rich river soil. Men work with their hands to break the lumps of earth with mauls and finish their task with wooden-toothed harrows. Seeds come from the previous year's crop and the first shoots of the plant spring up within several days.

The jute has to be weeded and thinned and takes about four months of care until the plants flower at a height of up to eighteen feet and are ready for cutting. Much of the success of the crop depends on the trade winds that bring spring showers to prepare the land for plowing and the June monsoons that swell the rivers so the jute may steep in them to soften.

Natives working waist-deep in the murky water cut the jute by hand as the rivers rise. They bundle it and put it in slow-moving pools, tying weights to the jute to hold it under the water. After about a week in the "retting" pool, it has softened enough so the outer bark can be stripped off by hand to expose the layer of fiber.

Standing in the pools, the natives loosen the fiber by beating it against the water. They rinse it in clear water, air and dry it in the sun, and hand-comb it before rolling it into bundles. Warehousemen at the major ports collect and sort the fiber and put it into 400-pound bales. The baling is done under such great pressure that when jute reaches American ropemakers it is in the form of a woody mass. It takes much careful preparation before it can be spun into twine and rope.

There are more than twenty synthetic fibers that have been tried for making rope. Some are still being tested and others, while proven useful, have been found to cost too much to be of practical value. Newer ones are under constant research and further rope uses for present man-made fibers are being developed every day. Half a dozen synthetic fibers already have become standard materials of ropemaking and their use is growing enormously.

Synthetic ropes generally are used for special purposes when there is some definite advantage to using them instead of less expensive natural fiber ropes. The most popular synthetics are based on chemical derivatives of coal or oil. Each has qualities the others lack, as well as faults, so that the choice of a synthetic rope must be judged carefully by the work it is to do.

Nylon lines, size for size, are nearly twice as strong as those of natural fiber. They wear two to four times as long, have about four times the working elasticity, and are easy to keep clean with fresh water and hand scrubbing. Nylon's stretch under sudden strain and ability to absorb shock makes it especially suitable for safety rope and for certain kinds of loading. Its loss of strength is small when wet or frozen and, since there is no swelling, it runs through blocks and pulleys when wet as easily as it does when it is dry.

It resists abrasion, mildew and rot and underwater borers that attack rope in sea water, stands up well to most common solvents and chemicals, and isn't much damaged by oil or grease. But nylon rope is affected by drying oils, such as the linseed oil used by painters, and by some mineral acids. And for some kinds of work, nylon is considered too slippery.

Basically, there are two kinds of nylon rope, filament nylon and spun nylon. The filament rope is sleek and silky in appearance and is made from continuous filaments that run as unbroken threads for the entire length of the rope. Spun nylon, made from short staple lengths of nylon fiber, is not quite so strong or smooth. But it is easier to handle when wet and it knots and splices more readily.

Nylon fiber is produced from coal, water and air through a series of chemical changes that convert it to a solution which is blended again and again, melted and ejected, and finally drawn into a material that emerges as a single yarn. It sometimes is pre-twisted and several ends are piled together.

So as to overcome the crystal-like nature of the yarn, it is drawn between rollers that revolve at several different speeds. These stretch it many times its original length and make the tough elastic fiber which is wound on tubes to be delivered to the ropemaker. The same machines that make natural fiber ropes lay this into nylon filament rope.

For spun rope, nylon tow is used. It is broken into lengths of about eight or ten inches on special machinery. Dacron, another of the same general family of synthetics, has many of the qualities of nylon and is laid into either filament or spun ropes. Although not quite so strong, it has special features that make it better for some marine and fishing uses. Wet or dry, it stretches somewhat less than nylon, keeps rigid and absorbs less water.

Polyethylene fibers, chemically processed from petroleum, air and sometimes salt brine by creating gases that are converted to liquid and resins, are made into a wide range of ropes in various sizes and colors. The resins pass through carefully controlled heating cylinders that change them into a soft mass that can be extruded somewhat like toothpaste from a tube. Heating, scientific stretching, and exact cooling develop a filament that is wound on spools ready for making plastic rope.

They have a glassy smooth appearance and are nearly as strong as nylon, are light and flexible, resist acid and rot and are waterproof. But they don't wear so well as some other kinds of rope under friction because they melt at high temperatures. However, polyethylene ropes have very special qualities in the fact that they float and take permanent coloring.

Water skiers have found that bright yellow polyethylene rope is seen easily on the water and that its floating helps retrieve upset skiers and also keeps the rope from being caught in the boat's propeller. It also is widely used for roping off swimming areas, for buoy lines, and for emergency rope barriers on land. Yellow and black polyethylene ropes that show good visibility at night as well as during the day are put around road and building excavations and as barriers to hold back crowds at fires or accidents.

Glass fiber ropes are used mainly on work where very high temperature resistance is needed. But they are not very flexible, not so good when wet, and are less common in general use than ropes made of the other synthetic fibers.

Most of the synthetic materials can be made into braided as well as twisted rope, especially in the smaller sizes. Because they often are stronger than natural fiber ropes, smaller ones frequently serve where a larger natural rope would be required.

For the makers of twisted rope, the synthetic fibers eliminate a major step in manufacture, since the man-made yarns or filaments come to them ready to spin and don't have to be specially prepared.

With natural fibers, the first step in modern ropemaking is the careful preparation. Fibers of many kinds and grades, stored in the huge warehouse, are sampled and laboratory tested so that expert blenders may go to work. They put together a little of one grade with some of another to create a mixture exactly suited to a rope that will serve some particular use.

Handfuls of these blended fibers, called "heads," are then put on the feeders of the 30-foot-long machines known as "breakers." The machines are in two sections, each with an endless chain of steel bars studded with hackle pins and moving at different speeds to set up a combing action between them.

Rows of moving combs work over the fiber to lay the ends parallel and to combine them. This forms an endless band or "sliver" of fiber. It goes through six or eight more treatments of mechanical combing, slimming and combining until the final sliver is ready for spinning into yarn.

During all of this, the fiber passes under an oil spray which softens, lubricates and helps to waterproof it. Special treatments of various cordage oils, waxes or formula chemicals may be applied. They may be needed for mooring or fishing lines to be used underwater, rope used in the damp tropics or freezing Arctic, or under conditions where it has to resist unusual industrial chemicals, vegetable growth, bugs or insects.

Rope usually isn't given any special treatment because for ordinary uses it will wear out in service before it comes apart for any other reason. If it is well-made and lubricated to lessen interior and surface friction, there is normally no need for a preservative.

Anything applied to the rope by hand after it leaves the factory may do more harm than good. Hand dippings, oil soakings, waxing or tarring seldom penetrate to the inner yarns of the rope when tried on a do-it-yourself basis. Instead of protecting rope, they add unnecessary weight and may cause friction or other damage with the useless coating of the surface. The safe rule, if special rope is needed, is to buy it factory-treated. Rope with regular lubrication and waterproofing is called "plain."

Spinning is the next step in manufacture. Piled coils of blended and prepared slivers are fed to an automatic spinning machine called a "jenny." This gives the fibers the required number of turns to twist them into finished yarn and draws the yarn through to wind itself on a large bobbin.

During the spinning, the yarn must be kept to an exact weight, strength, smoothness and uniform size. Constant testing also measures the amount of twist. There must be just enough to keep the fibers from slipping under tension, but not too much twist or it would reduce the strength of the yarn. It may be sold in this form as single-yarn binder and baler twines or carried along in the further process of making rope.

Bobbins of yarn are delivered to various finishing departments to make tying twines of several yarns or different kinds of rope. For standard rope, the bobbins are next placed on a rack of horizontal steel pegs, the number of bobbins depending on the size of the strand that is to be formed.

The ends of yarn are led through regularly spaced holes of what is known as a "face plate" and drawn together through a steel forming tube. By compressing them and twisting them in the opposite direction from which the yarn itself was spun, this forms the yarns into a strand. It is drawn onto a revolving wheel in a way that regulates the twist.

Laying the rope is the final operation. When the strands have been formed and coiled on reels, the big reels are hoisted by an electric crane to be fitted into place on a "layer" machine. This twists three or more strands, in an opposite direction from which the strands themselves were formed, to lay them into one complete rope.

The huge machine does its twisting with great speed by drawing the strands through a block or die of the correct size and winding the finished rope on giant reels. It takes precision engineering to gear the machines for each type of rope to be made and skill to set them so the rope twists evenly, with a steady pace and a uniform tension on each of the strands.

Standard rope, known as "plain-laid," is made of three strands. There is also four-strand and occasionally six-strand rope and some of it has a core or "heart." Adjusting the machines for harder or softer twisting produces ropes of varied tensile strength or construction that withstands certain forms of bending, fatigue and strain, all determined by the specific job that rope is engineered to perform.

Making cables involves still another step in which three complete ropes of three strands each are laid together. Once again, they are twisted in a direction opposite to which each of the ropes was made. People sometimes mistakenly call any thick rope a "cable," but it isn't one unless it is a rope made of ropes rather than strands. Giant cables occasionally may be twenty-five inches around or more.

Cord and rope made of cotton usually are braided rather than twisted and generally are kept to sizes of less than an inch in diameter. They should not be used for jobs requiring heavier rope. However, when put to the purposes for which it is made, good quality braided cotton rope is long-wearing and easy on the hands.

Braided rope cannot be spliced. It also tends to come apart on the surface more easily than twisted rope. But it may serve even better than twisted rope in some cases when a twist complicates the work that has to be done. A twisted rope that is being used for something that is circling around constantly, for instance, may tend to unlay its strands or give a crooked turn to the rope or to what it is holding.

Cotton fiber is prepared for cordmaking much in the way that threads are made for textile uses. The yarn is made from raw cotton by carding, combing, drawing and spinning operations. Many threads are spun into the compact yarn in whatever strength is desired. A number of these yarns are then braided or woven into cord.

Lower grades of cotton rope use coarse yarn or strands of "roving" instead of yarn. The roving, made in a process preliminary to spinning, is loosely twisted cotton material. It is formed into a large single strand in place of a strand made up of numerous separate yarns. Sometimes cheaper ropes are "loaded" with materials or chemical treatment to give them extra bulk or weight.

Better cotton ropes are the hollow-braided or solid-braided types, the construction being as important as the quality of the fiber. Hollow-braided cord is less apt to stretch or twist than other types, but often doesn't wear so well as the solid-braided type in use over pulleys or when there is other friction.

Wire rope is the strongest of all ropes. It is formed of steel wires wound on a fiber core or on a core of smaller wire rope. The type of the core and the size of the individual wires determine the rope's strength and flexibility. Fiber core makes the wire rope more flexible, but steel core gives greater strength.

There are several kinds of steel wire used in making rope, the most common being of plow steel. Molten steel, white hot from the mill furnaces, is teemed into huge molds which are stripped off when the steel cools, leaving solid ingots. These ingots are lengthened and reduced in size at a "blooming mill" by being reheated and passed through big wringer-like rollers that squeeze as they turn them over and over.

When they are about two inches square and thirty feet long, the newly rolled sections, now called "billets," go to a rod mill to be heated once more to rolling temperature and started through a long series of reducing machines to produce rods of various sizes and uses. Then the rods are drawn through a number of dies of gradually diminishing size to the required gauge and the finished wire is twisted by great vertical rope machines, some of which weigh eighty tons.

The wires are wound together to form the strand in an arrangement that has a definite pitch and then twisted symmetrically around the core. In general, the larger the number of wires in a strand and the greater the number of strands, the more flexible the rope will be.

Hoisting ropes, for instance, must be flexible, so they usually are made of six strands of up to twenty-five wires in each strand, and with a fiber rope core. But such things as guy wires and highway guards do not have to be flexible and those may be made of a wire rope of six strands with only seven or eight wires in each strand.

When wire rope is wound on small drums under heavy loads, resistance to crushing is important so a wire core, rather than fiber, is used. For certain types of slings and on construction work with heavy equipment, the choice may be what is called "preformed" wire rope. This is less likely to set or kink and broken wires do not unravel so easily to cut the hands of men using it.

However, before handling any kind of wire rope, it is always wise to inspect it carefully for broken wires. And, just because wire rope is stronger than others, it doesn't follow that any wire rope will lift a heavy load safely. The right size for each job still must be chosen with care to avoid accidents.

Selecting the Right Rope

The rope you choose should depend on the needs of the job it has to do, how strong it must be, how durable and how flexible. Fiber, size and construction of the rope decide these qualities.

A rope's strength comes mainly from its size and the fibers used in making it. Some jobs obviously need stronger rope than others to lift a load or to pull a weight, so that strength may be the most important point to consider.

But durability may be more important for another type of work where the rope may be exposed to the friction of pulleys, winches or other things that will cause abrasion. The size and construction, as well as the kind of fiber, play a part in how well the rope will wear.

Flexibility may be the first need for safety and ease of work with blocks and tackle, slings, hoisting and towing or mooring. Construction of the rope, especially its lay and twist, has a lot to do with how flexible it is.

Sometimes it is necessary to decide which of two conflicting needs is more important. The experience of others who have used rope for somewhat the same work is the best guide to this. Any rope supplier or cordage manufacturer will be glad to suggest the kind most commonly used. Most classified phone books, or trade directories which may be found in the public library, list rope suppliers.

In addition to standard ropes, many special-purpose ropes have been developed over the years to meet the conditions of individual work or sports. These usually take their names from the type of work they do, such as *ski-tow rope, trawl line, truck rope, crab line, lariat rope* and so on. Most workmen and industries making regular uses of rope have selected certain kinds as best suited to various jobs.

Ropes with special types of preservative treatment usually have the name of the preparation that is used added to the name of the rope. This may be pine tar to keep out moisture, tallow or graphite for extra lubrication, or some copper-based compound to protect underwater rope against marine growth.

The special ropes meet unusual problems. A *high climber rope* was developed, for instance, for the lumbermen who climb tall trees to timber them by cutting off the tops. Many men were hurt using ordinary rope that accidentally was chopped in two by the swing of an axe. A rope with a hard wire core was made to guard against the axe slips that toppled them to the ground.

Ski tows brought the need for a rope that would resist the effects of water, ice, dirt and rocks, straining tension and summer storage and that also wouldn't stain the clothing of skiers. But even more important was the complaint that ordinary rope tended to twist or spiral on the tows, making it uncomfortable to hold and dangerous because scarfs, gloves or other loose clothing might wind around the rope. Ropemaking engineers found a way to balance the twist of the rope to neutralize it.

Crab fishermen wanted a line with a special lay that would let them part the strands so bait could be thrust between them and still hold firmly. Fishermen of all sorts probably are the most specialized users of rope, needing many types and treatments due to the variety of commercial fishing methods and the conditions they encounter in different places.

However, unless there is some very special requirement, the average user will choose a standard rope, of which there are more than fifty kinds in enough different sizes and weights to allow a wide selection that will serve most jobs well.

Size and Strength

The rope you choose should be about five times as strong as the heaviest load you expect it to take. Estimate the maximum working load to which the rope will be subjected and multiply that by five to determine what breaking strength will be required. In other words, if you are making a rope ladder, for example, you should use a rope with the breaking strength five times that of the heaviest person who will climb it.

Although that may seem to allow a very wide margin of safety, the five-to-one factor is considered standard rope practice. It not only gives extra protection against the parting of fibers due to sudden strains and shock, but also safeguards against unnecessary wear. Using undersized rope greatly increases internal stress on the fibers, so that it doesn't last so long or give as good service.

Even when nobody's personal safety or property depends on the strength of a rope, it is smart never to try to make a small rope do the work of a large one. A frayed or broken rope means time lost in replacing it, if nothing else.

Fiber rope often is sold by the pound instead of by the foot, except in small amounts which are sometimes pre-packaged. Size once was measured only by the circumference of the rope, but now both the circumference and diameter usually are given. When sailors mention the size of a rope, they generally are talking about how big it is around. Those who use it on land usually speak of size in terms of the diameter.

Still another way of measuring the size of smaller ropes is by the number of threads of yarn they contain. Thus, one rope may be designated as having 21 threads, being 1½″ in circumference, or ½ ″ in diameter, all meaning the same size. But there is no need for confusion, since manufacturers usually give all measurements in listing weights, strengths and the average number of feet to the pound for various sizes of rope.

A regular three-strand manila rope of ½ ″ diameter averages about thirteen feet of rope to the pound, has a breaking strength of about 2,650 pounds and can take a safe work load of about 530 pounds.

Specification charts which give this sort of information for other sizes and types of rope are available from rope suppliers. They vary, of course, according to the brand of rope and its materials. If you are buying a small amount of rope, probably your local hardware dealer or building supply company has a chart you can consult to check your needs.

Twist and Construction

The direction in which the strands are laid together to make the rope and how tightly they are twisted have a lot to do with the way a rope performs on the job.

Most rope has its strands twisted together to the right. This construction has become standard over a long period of time because it has been found best for the greatest number of uses.

Sometimes, however, the twisting sequence is reversed to make "left-laid" rope. This usually is used in connection with a length of right-laid rope so that the twists in the two ropes balance. In certain kinds of commercial fishing, for instance, a right-handed rope is used on one side of the net and a left-handed rope on the other and they compensate to keep the net from rolling up at the edges. Cables generally are made of ropes twisted together to the left.

The three standard degrees of twist are soft, medium and hard. A tightly twisted rope, called "hard-laid," resists abrasion better than medium twisted rope, but is stiff and has somewhat less strength. Softly twisted rope is stronger and easier to handle than medium-laid rope, but doesn't stand up so well to wear if it must rub against something. There are many other variations in the twisting to suit special purposes.

Rope construction, incidentally, often helps police solve crimes. Chemists in police laboratories of scientific crime detection study the lay and twist of strands, the angle of twist, stress of the fibers and such things as age and condition in order to identify rope found at the scene of a crime. Because it is so durable, rope often far outlasts other evidence.

There is no fiber that cannot be identified, so that even a few splinters of rope may help, and all fibers are distinctive under chemical tests and microscopes. Police keep a large index file of samples made by various rope companies to pin down the locality in which the rope was bought.

Cotton Cords

The sizes of cotton cord usually are given in numbers that indicate the diameter in thirty-seconds of an inch.

A number 7 cord is $\frac{7}{32}''$ in diameter, for instance, while a number 8 has a diameter of $\frac{1}{4}''$ and a cotton rope an inch in diameter would be size 32. Stock sizes of cotton cords for most uses run from 4 to 12 and cotton ropes from 14 to 24.

While cotton cord is sold by net weight at wholesale, the retail price of smaller quantities is by the foot. Standard hanks are one hundred feet each, two hanks being connected. It also is sold in coils or on wooden reels in 1,200 feet lengths, except for the very large sizes which are in coils half that length.

Wire Rope

Sizes of wire rope are identified by their diameter and by a set of paired numbers that indicate the number of strands in the rope and the number of wires in a strand.

For example, a 6 x 7 wire rope of any given diameter would have six strands of seven wires each. The first number in the pair designates the strands and the second the wires in each strand.

The diameter and strength of wire rope are governed by the type of core used, whether wire or fiber, and by the strength of steel of the individual wires. Wire ropes cannot be knotted readily and while they may be spliced, they usually are fastened with U-shaped or L-shaped metal clips.

Uncoiling a New Rope

If rope is to last and to give good service, it should be handled with the care that would be given a new tool from the day it is bought. Uncoiling it properly will avoid kinks that sometimes spread the strands and impair its wearing qualities.

Lay the wrapped coil flat on the floor with the inside end of the rope at the bottom. Don't remove the wrapping entirely, but open it enough to make sure which end is up. Leaving the wrapping around it will help keep the rope clean until all of it has been used.

With a sharp knife, reach into the center of the coil and cut the twine that holds the rope. Remove this so the rope will draw out freely. Now reach down through the center to the bottom and pull the tag end of the rope up through the coil. If it is standard right-laid rope, it should be uncoiled from the center in a counter-clockwise direction.

Do this slowly and carefully until you have removed the amount wanted and then cut it off cleanly with the knife. Thicker rope may be cut by placing it on a chopping block and using a hatchet.

Synthetic rope usually comes on reels. Unlike natural fiber rope, this should not be uncoiled from the center. The reel should be taken from its carton and the rope drawn straight off the reel. The reel may be put on a rod or spindle to revolve so the rope can be drawn off without kinking or tangling.

Preparing It for Use

A new rope may need some straightening before it can be used. One way to straighten a short length of rope is to hang it from a high place and attach a light weight at the bottom. But a better way is to work it carefully with the hands, gently adding or removing a little twist, as need be.

Proper uncoiling should avoid kinks, but if any develop they should be removed by easy twisting before the rope is put to use. Don't pull the rope to straighten out kinks. Unwind them properly by hand.

Kinks should be avoided in use as well as in preparing a new rope because they can cause permanent damage by destroying the lay of the rope. Remember that a rope is made of opposite twists and that it will be thrown out of balance if it is twisted repeatedly in one direction, such as in use over a pulley or when it spins with a free load attached to it. You can restore the balance by twisting it in the opposite direction.

Many tricks have been tried to straighten and flex new rope for use, but among those to be avoided are boiling it in water, pulling it around a rough tree, or dragging it along a road, on sand, or over cultivated land or paving. All such stunts injure the fibers.

A long rope may be straightened by dragging it across a smooth pasture or meadow, or by letting it trail gently through the water from the rear of a boat. However, most new rope will adjust itself to use with a little careful handling, without the need for elaborate working over.

The Care and Handling of Rope

Men who use rope regularly as a daily part of their jobs take pride in their skill in handling it, just as any good worker does in handling the tools long experience has taught him to use well. While most of us never expect to become rope experts, we can get more pleasure and longer use from rope by learning a few simple things about its care.

Old-time sailors sometimes used to tell boys new aboard ship that a man should treat a rope as he would a fellow human, think of it as being alive, and that would give him the common sense to keep from abusing it. Natural fiber ropes do, of course, come from living matter, the plants that produced them, so perhaps it isn't really too far-fetched to think of them as vegetable, if not human. Like vegetables, if they are treated roughly and not given proper care, they bruise, decay or rot.

Perhaps the first rule to follow in using rope properly is to avoid sudden jerks or strains on it whenever possible. If you take a piece of string in your fingers, you can see for yourself how hard it is to break with an even pull, but how quickly it will break with a sudden snap.

This same principle applies to rope. Sudden jerks on tow ropes, lashings, tackles or slings may cause breaks, or at least damage that could be avoided with a steady even pull. A suddenly dropped weight may jerk a line in two, while the same line would hold a far heavier weight that was let down on it slowly and easily.

Rope used to hoist anything that bends it at a sharp angle, such as the edges or corners of a heavy square box or piece of furniture, should have padding between it and the edge it bends across. Angular bends put great strain on the outer fibers of a rope. Folded cloth rags will serve as pads.

The outer fibers, as much as the inner ones, give rope its strength, so it is wise to eliminate as much surface wear as you can by seeing to it that the rope doesn't rub over splintered wood, rough or sharp metal, or places that are gritty. Rope dragged on the ground sometimes picks up gravel or small stones that become embedded between its strands and shorten its life.

Pulleys or metal sheaves used with rope should be inspected regularly to make sure they haven't worn to a sharp edge which may cut it. It is important that pulleys be the proper size to fit the rope so it rides well within the grooves. Block and tackle ropes, and those used on other jobs where one part of the rope gets more wear than the rest, should be reversed end for end every so often to give all sections equal wear.

In rainy weather, rope fixed between objects outdoors should be loosened. Guy lines or ropes used as other supports exposed to the weather should be slacked off or they may damage not only the rope but also what it is supporting. When rope is wet, it should be hung in the shade to dry, if possible, and also be kept from freezing in the cold. If ice does form on rope, use extra precaution in handling it. Sharp ice may cut rope fibers and also cut fingers that are holding it.

Ropes used aboard small boats sometimes are damaged by acid from storage batteries. If left lying around a garage floor, the oil and grease drippings from a car may injure them. Cords used in a workshop should be kept well away from chemicals. When painting, try to keep the paint from splashing on rope and keep linseed oil and other drying oils away from it.

Dirty rope can be washed with clean water, but should be allowed to dry thoroughly before storing. If an otherwise good rope has a small section that has become worn or damaged, the section should be cut out and the rope spliced back together.

Before using an old rope for a new job, go over the whole length of it to check its condition thoroughly. Look for cuts and damages, flex it to make sure it still has stretch and pliability, twist it open and look inside to see if there is internal wear.

The inner yarns should be of good color and the fiber strong. Sometimes the outer appearance of a rope can be deceptive. If you are at all in doubt, cut a short piece from the end of the rope and take it apart for a closer look.

All fiber ropes gradually lose some of their strength with age and wear and ropes that are under a heavy load should be inspected frequently. When there is any element of personal safety involved, such as in climbing or in rigging scaffolds, even brand-new rope should be looked over for possible defects before it is put to use.

Remember that the breaking strength of rope is figured on the basis of *new* rope and that more of a safety margin should be allowed for a rope that has been used for some time. A rope that has been overloaded to more than three-fourths of its breaking strength probably has suffered permanent injury. Severe jerks and strains it may have had also should be taken into account. If a rope has had hard use on one job, double check it before putting it under maximum strain on another.

Coiling Rope and Storing It

When you have finished using a rope, it always should be coiled. This is not only a matter of neatness and of keeping it from being damaged as it might be if just left lying around, but coiling also helps preserve the rope's proper balance.

The correct method of coiling a standard right-laid rope is clockwise, to the right, or as sailors say, "with the sun." Sometimes, however, with new rope or one that has developed a reverse twist in use, right-hand coiling is difficult and the rope may tend to kink. In this case, it may be coiled the other way, counterclockwise, until this twist has been taken out. Cables, being left-laid, should be coiled to the left.

Sailors have many ways of coiling rope aboard ship, most of them developed to allow quick and easy use of the line when needed. The seaman's *straight coil* is made by starting with the end of the line that is secured and taking slack in it to lay a circle on the deck. Then additional slack circles of rope are laid on top, with kinks and turns kept out, until the entire line is coiled. Capsizing the coil, turning the whole thing over, will clear it for the line to run free.

The sailor *Flemishes* a line by making a small circle of free end and continuing to lay down circles around it, in one layer only, until the entire line is flat on the deck in what looks somewhat like a coiled clock spring.

He *flakes down* a rope by laying out the free end in a straight line and then turning back a loop to form a close flat coil and continuing to lay long coils on top of each preceding one.

But for all practical purposes of the average rope user, a plain loosely formed coil hung over a wall peg will do for storage. The end can be brought through the center and hitched or lightly knotted around the coil to keep it from unwinding on its peg.

The place of storage should be cool, dry and well-ventilated, not close to the heat of boilers or furnaces. Larger ropes may be coiled on a platform of wooden slats. Rope should be kept off the floor and never should be left out in direct sunlight or in damp, hot places, nor should it be stored away while it is wet.

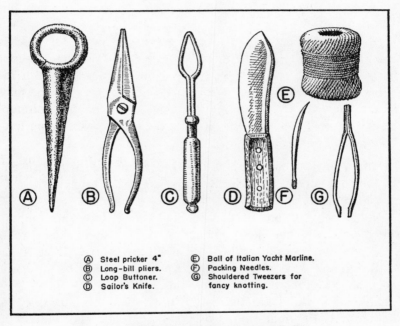

Ⓐ Steel pricker 4"
Ⓑ Long-bill pliers.
Ⓒ Loop Buttoner.
Ⓓ Sailor's Knife.
Ⓔ Ball of Italian Yacht Marline.
Ⓕ Packing Needles.
Ⓖ Shouldered Tweezers for fancy knotting.

SAILORS' ROPE TOOLS

3

Knots and Ties

THE TYING of knots is a skill as old as the use of rope itself, since a rope usually isn't much good as a tool unless it is tied to something.

Knots and ties are needed to haul, hoist, tow and support things and to fasten them together, as well as to shorten a rope or to join two ropes temporarily. There are well over three thousand different ways of tying rope. Knots are a part of the daily work of more than ninety occupations.

The sailor still leads the list of those who use knots. Even among early Egyptian sailors thousands of years ago, the art of knotting was highly developed. But knots were old before sailors first made them. Man learned to hunt and fish before he took to water in boats and he needed knots for his bows and traps and snares, for his fishlines and his nets.

Simple knots such as the Reef Knot, Overhand and Sheet Bend were part of everyday knowledge in the Stone Age. The ancient Lake Dwellers of Switzerland used the Sheet Bend to hold together the meshes of their nets. Some of the knots that surgeons use today in performing the latest operations of modern medical science, as well as knots that weavers and builders still use, are very old indeed.

Hobbyists who collect knots as others collect stamps and coins, trading each other bits of cord or diagrams of old and new knots and variations from all over the world, are avid searchers of the past. So are scientists who learn much from knots about the primitive peoples of the earth.

Some hobbyists collect occupational knots that have been passed from master to apprentice for centuries in almost every hand trade. They will stop a butcher or a tree-climber at work to have a new knot explained. Others specialize in the knots of heraldry, those used on the coats of arms of knights of old, or in fanciful ties such as Love Knots.

While all knots are simply ways of twisting cord, and all practical knots are ways of putting it to work, their legend parallels the story of man himself. The history of the first knots is so far lost in the dim reaches of time that nobody can more than guess at it. But it seems probable that the old Greeks and Romans, whose records do exist, may have known even more about tying knots than we do today. Some of the knots they describe are intricate wonders, the knack of which has long since been forgotten.

Knots are to be seen in many ancient works of art, often as part of the design of vases, represented in the tied girdles of the vestals of Rome and the intertwined strands of Mercury's staff. Since knots came long before there were locks, they were often a symbol of security in the tales of the ancients.

Homer, in the Odyssey, tells how Ulysses used "Circean art" in the crafty fastening of a mystic knot to secure the costly presents of golden vases, rich robes and other treasures that were a gift of Alcinoüs, king of the Phaeacians. According to the legend, the knot was so good nobody could untie it and only a single cord was needed to hold the valuables in safety against any who might try to seize them.

The celebrated Gordian Knot of Greek legend also supposedly

resisted the efforts of all those who sought to untie it. Back in the Fourth Century B.C., as the story goes, a Phrygian farmer by the name of Gordius became the chosen one of an oracle of Apollo and was taken from his fields to rule a small kingdom.

Gordius, in gratitude to the Olympian gods for his kingly promotion, hung up his plow in the temple of Jupiter as a votive offering. But he fastened one of the traces of the plow with a knot so cunning that nobody could find any loose end to undo it. Soon the oracles foretold that whoever freed the plow cord would be ruler of all Asia.

The knot, without beginning or end, baffled all who attempted to discover its secret until, in his search for worlds to conquer, Alexander the Great came upon it. He, too, was puzzled, but when he couldn't untie it, he lifted his mighty sword and severed the knot with a single bold and contemptuous stroke. The legend has given our language the proverbial phrase "to cut the Gordian Knot," or to solve some difficult matter by a bold, quick action such as Alexander used to slash apart the knot Gordius had tied.

Many attempts have been made by knot experts to guess what kind of knot farmer Gordius might have made. Some believe the plow trace wasn't knotted, but spliced so that the ends didn't show. Others think it was some form of a Multi-strand Stopper Knot. Speculation about it is fun, but since the story is only a legend, it is more likely that there never really was a Gordian Knot.

People in many parts of the ancient world, and some in Scandinavia and the English Channel islands up until a generation or so ago, firmly believed in the superstition that witches and wizards could tie up the wind in knots. Wizards in Finland used to sell charmed knots to mariners whose ships were becalmed.

The wizard would tie three knots in a rope, supposedly ensnaring the wind. A stranded mariner undid the first of the knots if he wanted a mild breeze to spring up to fill his sails. If he wanted more speed, the undoing of the second knot was promised to bring a half-gale. But woe unto the man who loosed the third charmed knot, except against an enemy, because that knot was bewitched to release a roaring hurricane.

Simple peasants in old Estonia, separated from Finland only by an arm of the sea, blamed the Finnish wizards for the bitter winds that blew from the north in the spring, bringing them colds and rheumatism. They feared to venture from their homes on certain days of the year because of the superstition that the knot-released winds might smite them dead.

Old women in Shetland and on the Isle of Man used to sell sailors knotted handkerchiefs to rule the storms with a similar set of three magic knots. In long-ago Greece, Plato warned in writing his *Laws* that the death penalty should be meted out to any person "who seems the sort of man who injures others by magic knots or enchantments." And in the far-off Alaska of an entirely different civilization, Eskimos made ropes of knotted seaweed to go down to the beaches and strike out against the winds.

Magic knots have played an important part in the superstitions of people of all ages. Priests serving the Roman god Jupiter were forbidden to have knots on any part of their garments. Moslem pilgrims on their way to Mecca were not allowed to wear knots. In parts of Europe up through the 1700's, it was believed that secretly tying certain knots near a person would bind him under a spell that would keep him from moving his body.

The French parliament at Bordeaux in 1718 sentenced a man to die after he was accused of spreading desolation through a whole family by means of knotted cords. During the same period in Scotland, two people were condemned to death for stealing charmed knots an old crone had made.

In the Koran there is a reference to the mischief of those who "puff into the knots," and there is an Arabian tale that the prophet Mohammed himself once was bewitched by an enemy who tied nine knots in a string which he then hid in a well. The story tells how Mohammed fell ill until the knots were found and undone to the chant of spells, each released knot gradually restoring his strength.

Russian brides sometimes wore a fishnet, made of many knots, over their wedding gowns to ward off the harm that might be cast by sorcerers. Superstitious Russian farmers not too many years ago used to think they could charm away wolves that might attack cattle by tying a bag over the head of one of the cows with a magic knot that was supposed to bind the jaws of any wolf that happened along.

Some African tribes thought knotted grass would help them catch people who tried to run away. They tied knots in the grass at the sides of footpaths, believing they could bind up the paths with magic to keep the fugitive from doubling back over them. It often worked because the runaway believed in the same superstition and was afraid to use the knotted paths for his escape.

Many are the legends of charmed knots to cure illness. In parts of Italy and Greece, a thread was knotted around the neck of a sick person overnight. The next morning, friends of the one who was ill would remove the thread and go to a hillside to tie it around a tree branch, thinking to transfer the sickness to the tree. But the patient had to be careful not to pass that particular tree again or else the fever supposedly would break loose from the tied branch and attack him.

What must have been a medical treatment of no easy task is described by Pliny the Elder, the old Roman naturalist who died while later investigating the volcanic eruption of Vesuvius. In one of the thirty-seven volumes of his *Natural History,* written in the first century to catalog all the then-known laws of the universe according to his beliefs, Pliny tells of tying nine knots in the strand of a spider's web. The tiny strand of knots was then tied to the person who was ill. But to make the cure work, the spell-maker had to name some widow as each of the knots was tied.

Pliny also said that if the bandages put on a wound were tied with a "Hercules Knot," the wound would heal more rapidly. The Romans gave that name to what we know as the common Reef Knot, because they thought Hercules invented it.

Knots are often known by more than one name, especially when they are used for different purposes, and the names don't help much in trying to learn where they first came from since almost all the basic knots were used by many people before various names were given to them.

Among the first books in English to mention by name some of the knots long in use by sailors, for instance, was Captain John Smith's *Sea Grammar,* not published until 1627. In that earliest of the manuals of seamanship, the famous leader of the Virginia Colony, who was saved from death by Pocahontas, listed the three knots most used by seamen as the Wall Knot, Bowline and Sheepshank.

The word "knot" itself, of course, stands for the sailor's measurement of a ship's speed. Back in the days when a "log" was used as a ship's speedometer, as it still is today on small ships and sailing craft, a line measured off in spaced knots told how fast it was traveling. Although most modern vessels compute speed from the revolutions of the propeller, a "knot" still means one nautical mile, approximately 6,077 feet, per hour.

It was about the 16th century when sailors generally began to measure speed with the log, a contrivance that included a chip of wood and a line, and a reel and sandglass for sand to trickle through to give the time. The log chip was triangular, with a weighted wooden base so it would stand upright in the water when it was cast off the stern of the ship. Attached to it was the log line, about 150 fathoms (six feet to a fathom) long, which was wound on the long reel.

The line had sixty feet or so of slack to let the chip fall well clear of the vessel before the speed was taken. Then there was a piece of colored bunting tied to the line and the rest of it was marked off by knots tied a fraction more than 47' 3" apart. When the log chip was tossed to bob upright in the water, the line would start to unreel and as soon as the rag that was tied around it appeared, the time was counted.

As the knots passed, they were counted until the sand in the log glass had run out. The number of knots on the line that were counted in 28 seconds was equal to the speed of the ship through the water. Ships from the 18th century on kept records of the log findings, along with all other important events of the voyage, in the log book that became the ship's diary.

Knots also helped the sailor find out how deep the water was beneath his ship by means of soundings taken with a lead-weighted line, called a "hand lead," that was lowered over the side. The line was marked off with knots or tied strips of rag in measurements of fathoms and the attached weight sometimes was hollowed out so wax could be put in the cavity to pick up particles of mud or sand when the weight touched bottom.

The leadsman, who took the soundings in those days before depth was measured by machine, stood on a platform that projected from the side of the ship. He held the weighted line by a toggle stick close to the end and swung it in a full circle above his head a couple of times before releasing it with enough momentum to carry it far forward. As it settled in the water, slack was taken in until the leadsman felt it touch bottom. When the ship came opposite it, so the line stretched straight up and down, the sounding knots were read and called out to the bridge.

Author Samuel Clemens, who was a Mississippi riverboat pilot before the Civil War, took his pen name from the traditional soundings with the knotted rope. He was then in Nevada during the silver mining boom, writing newspaper articles for the *Virginia City Enterprise,* when he decided to sign them "Mark Twain," the old Mississippi leadsman's call for the depth of two fathoms.

The knots that were used in heraldry are called "badges," and were ornaments of interlaced cordage or part of embroidered personal and family emblems. Warrior knights of 13th-century Europe had the emblems on a surcoat they wore over their chain mail armor and this was the coat that became known as a "coat of arms." Some of the curious and fanciful knots on old Celtic and Anglo-Saxon coats of arms were purely geometric ornaments, but others had a sign-language meaning.

Heraldic knots were used as insignia even before they became adapted as part of the later and more elaborate emblems on shields and coats of arms. The Wake Knot, which looks somewhat like a criss-crossed Figure Eight, was the badge of the brave Saxon leader, Hereward the Wake, who refused to submit to William the Conqueror in 1066. Now known to us as the Carrick Bend, its main practical use is for joining large ropes in a way that doesn't injure the rope when pulled taut.

The badge of Staffordshire was a plain Overhand Knot, while two open Granny Knots decorated the mantlings of noblemen of the Bouchier family. Other badges portrayed the union of two families or represented such mottoes as "Fast, though untied." Pope Leo X had an emblem with a twisted knot and a band around a yoke. The House of Savoy took a Figure Eight Knot for their device, with the motto, "It bends, but constrains not."

Bakers and pretzel-makers, incidentally, adopted the Figure Eight as one of the knots they used in making some varieties of twisted breads and cooked goods. While the knots of most pretzels are now stamped out by machine, American pretzel-makers, especially in the area around Lancaster, Pennsylvania, were adept at tying the dough by hand. Using the plain Overhand Knot as well as the Figure Eight, they could tie pretzels for special occasions that were sometimes nearly a foot long.

Some of the knots used in English family emblems were variations of the True Lover's Knot, which has many forms, including the Carrick Bend and simple Bowknot, so that it can't really be identified as any one knot we know today. But many were the stories and old English ballads written about it, such as the 16th century ballad of *Fair Margaret and Sweet William,* from whose graves grew a rose and a brier as high as the church top until "they could grow no higher, and they grew in a True Lover's Knot, which made all souls admire."

Legend had it that the True Lover's Knot "once tied by the tongue cannot by teeth be untied," meaning that its charm would hold the spoken vows of love safe from the anger of any who tried to part the couple. A signet ring said to have belonged to William Shakespeare, which was part of a collection preserved at Stratford-on-Avon, was engraved with a True Lover's Knot entwining the letters "W.S."

Knots were worn as shoulder insignia by officers of the United States Army. Regimental officers of the cavalry troops who helped protect settlers of the frontier West had the fringed epaulettes of their uniforms replaced in 1872 by shoulder knots of flat braid to help designate their rank.

For thousands of years, almost everywhere in the world where there has been cord or rope, people have tied knots to help them count, tell time, keep records, and to remember things. Sometimes the knot-tying device is a simple one, such as a string tied around a finger or a knot in the corner of a handkerchief as a reminder not to forget something that should be done.

But knotted cords also have been used to keep the accounts and the history of vast nations, to serve as calculators for mathematical problems, and as a substitute for writing itself. As a memory device somewhat akin to a prayer chain, Indian wampum string or a set of Chinese counting beads, knots have helped ancient story-tellers recall the past glories of a race. They have been personal diaries and also what amounted to blueprints of memory for the builders of roads, bridges and temples.

Egyptian hieroglyphics show that looped and knotted cords were a familiar memory device before the pyramids were built. And before the early Chinese had any form of writing, they kept records with a conventional system of tying knots.

There is a Chinese legend that it was back about 2800 B.C. that Emperor Fu-hi invented written symbols to replace the knotted cords. He is said to have created a system of straight and broken lines to symbolize the knots and to stand for such basic things as heaven, water, boundary, wood and earthquake. Later, other sages improved the pictures in the form of birds' claws and that supposedly led to the real start of Chinese writing.

Modern language scholars sometimes dispute the theory that

the bird claws had anything to do with it and believe that the first symbols were merely pictures, such as a circle with a dot in the center to represent the sun. But however writing came about, the old Chinese apparently were reluctant to trade their knotted cords for a written language.

Confucius wrote that some people who were never satisfied with new inventions would like to turn back to previous ways of doing things and that there were those who would "induce people to return to the old custom of knotted cords and to use them in place of writing." One of the books attributed to Confucius tells of the legend itself: "In the highest antiquity, knotted cords were used for the administration of government. During the following century, the saintly man Fu-hi replaced these by writing."

In later years, Chinese philosophers sometimes likened knots to the various stars in the constellations and tried to calculate the position of stars with a system of knots. The symbolism of knots also was highly developed in the insignia on the military uniforms of ancient Chinese war lords.

Many people have used knots as a simple way of counting days. Early Greek warriors left to guard a bridge while other units of an army advanced sometimes were given leather thongs with a number of knots in them equal to the number of days they were to continue their watch over the bridge.

In India, guests invited to a festival often received their invitation in the form of a knotted string to mark the days before the event would take place. Each guest cut one knot from his string every day and when only one remained, they all assembled on the proper day. Native merchants in other parts of India sometimes kept an account of money due them by knotting a grass string which they wore tied around the back of their hair.

Sailing days in the Caroline Islands of the Pacific in the 1700's were reckoned with a knotted cord and the Samoans tied knots in the top leaves of coconut trees to mark the passing days. Natives of Formosa, with no other way to keep time, did it by knotting reeds. And native wives of the Guianas knotted strings when their husbands went away on trips and used them as calendars to tell when their men would return.

Tax collectors in Hawaii years ago used a rope four hundred fathoms long as a "revenue book." It was marked off in sections to correspond to various districts of the island. The native treasury men used knots, loops and tufts of cord of different shapes, colors and sizes to keep an accurate record of the hogs, pigs or pieces of sandalwood gathered as taxes from each family.

North American Indians also used knots for calculating dates. If the men of two tribes wished to meet on some future day, each would take a piece of string with a matching number of knots to untie so as to keep the appointment on time. Knot diaries were kept by Yakima Indian women to remember the important things that had happened during their lives. Some were strings up to thirty-five feet long, with weeks marked in groups of seven knots, and with other knots between for the events they wished to recall.

The Iroquois Indians kept records of tribal legends and history by means of knotted strings and arrangements of light and dark bands. Certain men of the tribe were assigned to memorize the full meaning represented by each string and they became somewhat like living libraries, able to recite important happenings of the past whenever they were called on to finger the cords of memory.

Indians of New Mexico used knotted strings in 1680 to spread word to all the pueblos of the date fixed for an uprising against the Spaniards. In later times, the Paloni Indians of California sent blanket salesmen equipped with calculating devices made of twisted hair rope to the settlement of San Gabriel.

Sheep herders in Bolivia and in the valleys of the Andes still use knot figuring to count their flocks. And during the 1800's, several attempts were made in Europe to introduce knot alphabets for the use of the blind, various knot groupings standing for letters of the alphabet, so reading might be done by passing the cords through the hands. This idea, however, proved to be too complicated to be practical.

But the most amazing of all the users of knots were the Incas of Peru, who ruled for thirteen generations over what became one of the greatest empires on earth. Their dominions reached from the plains of the Amazon to the Pacific, an area equal to the size of the whole United States east of the Rocky Mountains. Sometimes called the "Romans of the Western Hemisphere," the Incas themselves were a small group of people who, by their superior ability, brought the other peoples around them into a union of one government.

The Incas ruled as absolute monarchs over a highly complex system of small states, ended wars and adopted social laws to benefit the people, introduced great land reforms to make the most use of the farms that supported the nation, constructed irrigation canals, bridges and other public works. They built rich temples, traveled in splendor, developed the arts and created a high civilization.

All of this they did without a written language. The Incas were a people with a wealth of tradition and culture and a richly expressive spoken tongue, but they had no system of writing at all, not even a form of picture writing such as that of the Egyptians or Chinese whom they rivaled in the genius of their works and knowledge. What they had instead were knotted cords, called "quipus."

These were never a substitute for written language in the sense that the knots stood for letters of the alphabet or for words, but the Incas made the quipu into one of the most remarkable recording devices man has known. With their knotted ropes, they kept records of almost everything that went on anywhere in their far-flung empire. The quipus were used to send messages, take regular census reports, collect taxes, keep records of crops and herds, tools and clothes, houses and buildings, and accounts of nearly everything that everybody did, from one day to the next and year to year.

Cotton and wool of llamas and other animals were used by expert Peruvian weavers and ropemakers to form cords that have lasted well-preserved through the centuries. Some of them were vegetable-dyed with vivid colors that resisted the fading of time. Many quipus have been found, some buried with the Inca dead as their most important tools, so that present-day scientists have been able to piece together their fascinating story.

Usually natural white or buff in color, the main cords were formed by spinning yarns twice the length that was desired, doubling them back with a loop at one end, and then twisting the two strands together and tying off the free end with a knot.

Each quipu had one main horizontal cord, which might be anything from a few inches up to forty inches or more in length. Hanging down from this, as from a stretched-out clothesline, were a number of tied-on vertical cords. These were seldom more than twenty inches long, but there could be from two or three to a hundred or more.

With these, they used a decimal system counted in rows of knots that started at the bottom of each string. A single Overhand Knot at the bottom indicated the number "one." If it was in the next row up, it stood for "ten," and in the row above that, "one hundred," and so on.

Frequently, there was a Figure Eight Knot, instead of the Overhand, or a long knot formed like a closed fist, to indicate that units of the same order were being repeated and thus avoid a cluster of small knots. If a loop was pulled through and drawn taut, it was like the bookkeeper's red line to show that an account was closed.

Hanging strings of certain colors were used to represent time ahead or time past. Other colors apparently stood for districts of the empire, religions or trades. There were still different colors to indicate specific things, such as yellow ropes for gold, white for silver, green for grain.

A separate cord looped through the hanging strands along the top was knotted to show the sums of numbers or groups through

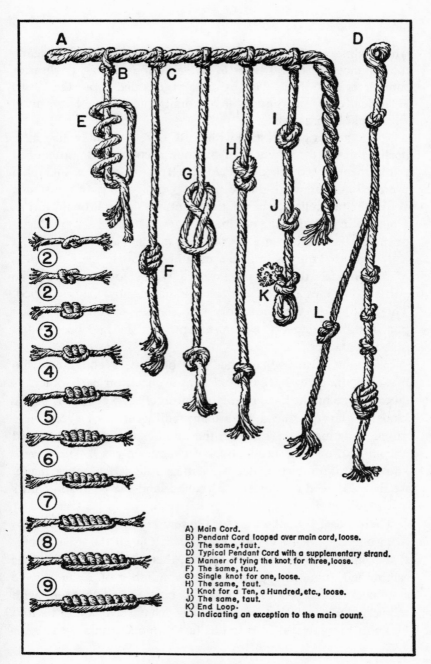

A) Main Cord.
B) Pendant Cord looped over main cord, loose.
C) The same, taut.
D) Typical Pendant Cord with a supplementary strand.
E) Manner of tying the knot for three, loose.
F) The same, taut.
G) Single knot for one, loose.
H) The same, taut.
I) Knot for a Ten, a Hundred, etc., loose.
J) The same, taut.
K) End Loop.
L) Indicating an exception to the main count.

INCA QUIPUS

from the collection in the Museum of Natural History

which it passed. This gave a record for a period of eight years, for instance, of several types of related things. Times of disaster sometimes were marked off by dark strands tied above the knots. Historical dates, astronomical reckonings and other large numbers could be preserved.

Some smaller quipus, tied with cords of red, possibly may have been demands for payment of overdue accounts that threatened punishment if the bill presented in terms of knots wasn't paid promptly. Others were the personal "books" of a man's business. When the tax collector came, the quipu would be brought out as a means of verifying the number of eggs that had been produced or the amount of expense for the feed of a horse.

Judges used quipus to give a monthly report to their superiors of the sentences they had pronounced, with colors to indicate the particular crimes and the number of knots to show the cases tried. Threads tied to the knots told whether the accused had been punished, and the sort of punishment, or if he had been found innocent and set free.

Each small Inca village had two or three accountants who recorded things with knots and kept a check on each other. A large village might have twenty or more. They kept track of the kinds of grain produced, how many bulls, calves or sheep were raised, how many slaughtered, the number of cows milked and not milked, and the production of cheese or wool. There were knot records of births, deaths, battles fought, speeches made, women widowed or children orphaned, and the passage of laws and regulations.

There was a system set up for the sending of speedy dispatches from one part of the empire to another. On all the great routes that connected with the Inca capital, there were small buildings established about five miles apart. A number of runners were stationed at each post to carry quipus back and forth, along with the verbal message that would explain whatever couldn't be told by knots or figurings. It wasn't as fast as modern mail service, of course, but the relay runners could carry their quipus at the rate of 150 miles a day.

Each district had Officers of the Knots, or officially appointed keepers of the quipus, who were given the title *Quipucamayus*. They were required to furnish the government with information on various important matters such as revenues, raw materials and supplies on hand.

Analysts also were appointed to go over the knot records and report on the general trends of affairs. There were historians who knotted cords to help them remember important events and to pass the history along to younger men who could learn it and repeat it by using the quipus to refresh their memories.

But the knots stood for numbers only and no historical event, the speech of an envoy or the reasoning of his arguments, could be expressed by them. Such things were preserved by means of short sentences, committed to memory, which gave the general meaning. The historians taught them to their successors and they were handed down from father to son.

Story-tellers, those who kept the legends and the fables in their minds, also used the knotted ropes to jog their memories. Knot scribes were called on frequently to repeat the information of the past, using the knots to go by, as a means of training so that meanings were never allowed to slip from mind.

Much of what we know about the quipus, in addition to the studies that have been made of the ropes themselves, is from the many writings of the scholars, jurists and priests who followed in the wake of the Spanish Conquest of South America in the 1500's that ended the rule of the Incas.

There are several collections of Inca quipus in the United States, including an excellently documented one at The American Museum of Natural History in New York. But the verbal stories that made the meaning of the knots clear to the Incas, the records they kept only in memory, have been lost.

Scientists know pretty well how the quipus were used, but the accounts they tell of a great ancient civilization can be only guessed. For the most part, the secrets of the Incas are still held by the knots their fingers tied centuries ago.

WORK KNOTS

ALTHOUGH most of us have been tying knots of one kind or another all our lives, few of us know how to tie them correctly. There are some basic knots that should be as much a part of everybody's knowledge as the ability to read and write.

They are not difficult to learn and a bit of fun practicing them now and then will give a good choice of practical ways to fasten cord or rope that will suit most purposes.

Beyond that, of course, there are all the specialized knots that serve some particular use instead of a general purpose. For those who wish to explore them in detail, such books as *The Ashley Book of Knots*, by Clifford W. Ashley, or *The Encyclopedia of Knots and Fancy Rope Work*, by Raoul Graumont and John Hensel, which may be available in the public library, contain literally thousands of knots and variations.

A knot should never be less than perfect, if it is to do its job. Every practical knot is meant to work in a certain way and if it isn't tied properly, it may act in a different way or simply fall apart. If one cord is crossed over another when it should be crossed under, the knot won't come out right. Unless the sequence is followed exactly, it will be entirely wrong.

Before you tie a knot, figure out what you want it to do. Several different knots might be used for the same job, depending on whether you want a more or less permanent tie, for example, or one that will untie easily for temporary use. Decide whether a rope is to fasten things together, lift them, pull them or whatever, and choose a knot accordingly.

Most knots should be worked into shape by easing them into position, not by giving a quick pull on the ends or the rope. Before using the rope, make sure the knot is securely in place. An improper knot, or one not drawn tight, causes unnecessary friction and may break. Ease weight or strain against a knot gently.

The sharp bends necessary to tie a knot weaken the fibers so that rope usually should be tied with the least number of bends possible. One good knot often is stronger than many. Two ropes knotted together end to end are only about half as strong as a single length of rope. Ropes should be spliced together, rather than knotted, for greater strength when the fastening is to be permanent.

A six-foot length of ¼″ diameter manila rope is excellent for practicing the tying of knots, since it has enough stiffness and body to hold their shape. However, Number 10 braided cotton cord also will hold its shape and is easier on the hands. A piece of string or even a round shoelace will do.

There are various methods of tying most standard knots, all of them right if they produce the wanted knot. You may have learned to tie some of them by methods different from those given here, but equally as good. The moves made in tying knots are mostly a matter of habit and use.

Whipping a Rope

The ends of a rope should be bound to keep them from unraveling. This can be done with freezer or friction tape, but the sailor does it by whipping the ends with twine.

For small rope, ordinary string or heavy thread may be used in place of twine. There are many ways of whipping a rope, but perhaps the simplest way is to start by putting a loop of twine against the side of the rope near the end to be whipped. The piece of twine should be a foot or two long and the end of it simply bent back to itself to make the small loop. Hold this against the side of the rope with the left thumb and wind the free end of twine tightly and firmly around both the loop and the rope. (See Plate Number 1.)

Make a dozen or so turns with it and then thread the end of the twine through the loop as you would thread a needle. Pull the other end of the loop so that the whole loop is drawn back about halfway beneath the whipping. Trim the ends of twine off close to the rope.

The Parts of a Knot

If you understand the terms that generally are used to describe the parts of a knot, it will make the knot ties easier to follow. (See Plate Number 1.) A knot has these three parts:

The *end*, as the name suggests, is the very end of the rope, the one being used to form the knot.

The *standing part* is the longest or main part of the rope, the part usually not being used in tying the knot.

The *bight* is the center part between them, curved by bending the end back toward the standing part.

In addition, these basic twists are given a rope in making knots:

An *overhand loop* is made by crossing the end *over* the standing part.

An *underhand loop* is made by crossing the end *under* the standing part.

A *turn* is taken when a rope is looped once around an object or itself.

A *round turn* is taken by looping a rope twice around an object.

Stopper Knots

Stopper Knots, which usually are tied to make a knot at the end of a rope to keep it from slipping out of a pulley or through a hole or the loop of another knot, include some of the more familiar knots most of us first learned to tie. Stoppers secure the end of a thread in sewing, provide hand-holds and foot-holds, add weight to the end of a rope that is to be thrown, and are used for decoration in rope crafts.

They sometimes also are used to keep the end of a twine or small cord from fraying. But rope or larger cord should be whipped or bound with tape to prevent fraying, not knotted.

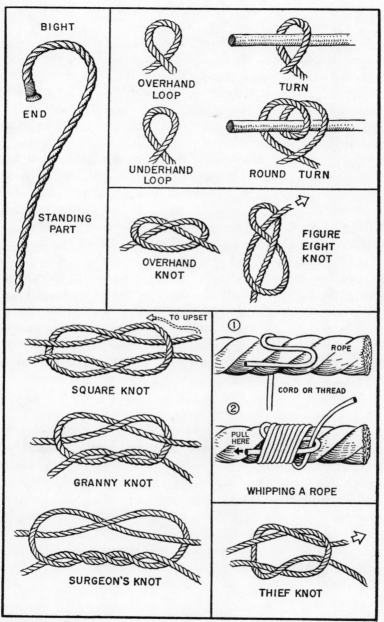

BIGHT

END

STANDING PART

OVERHAND LOOP

UNDERHAND LOOP

TURN

ROUND TURN

OVERHAND KNOT

FIGURE EIGHT KNOT

TO UPSET

SQUARE KNOT

GRANNY KNOT

SURGEON'S KNOT

① ROPE

CORD OR THREAD

② PULL HERE

WHIPPING A ROPE

THIEF KNOT

PLATE Nº1

An *Overhand Knot* (Plate Number 1), the simplest of the Stopper Knots, is one we all know how to make by forming an overhand loop and then passing the end under and out through the loop. It is the beginning of a number of other knots. The Overhand itself should be used mostly on twine and small cord, since it tends to jam larger ropes and becomes hard to untie and often injures rope fiber.

When the Overhand Knot is tied with one hand, as it is in sewing and sometimes in fastening packages, it is called a *Thumb Knot*. The string or thread is given a loose round turn around the tip of the forefinger and pushed off the finger with the thumb so that the end rolls through the turn. A pull on the standing part then forms the knot, usually under the tip of the second finger.

The *Double Overhand Knot*, sometimes called a *Blood Knot*, is formed by making a simple Overhand Knot and then merely passing the end under and out through the loop a second time before drawing it tight. A *Threefold Overhand Knot* may be made by giving the end still another turn before drawing the knot taut, but this is considered mainly a decorative knot, sometimes tied over a needle in embroidery work. The Double Overhand was used as a snapper at the end of the rope whip of the old-time ox driver.

A *Figure Eight Knot* (Plate Number 1) is the sailor's common Stopper Knot, tied aboard ship instead of the simple Overhand Knot because it is larger, stronger, easier to untie and doesn't have the same tendency to jam. It also is considered the best knot to use to keep the end of a rope from running out of a tackle or pulley and does less harm to rope fiber than the Overhand. Another name for it is the *Flemish Knot*. The Figure Eight may be tied by starting with an overhand loop. Then bring the end around over the standing part, pass it under and up through the loop, and draw it tight.

Binding Knots

Binding Knots are used to tie packages, to hold something together or hold it in place, or to bind two or more objects firmly to each other.

The commonest Binding Knot is the *Square Knot* or *Reef Knot* (Plate Number 1), which the sailor used for reefing and furling his sails. It is excellent for tying packages and bundles and is used in many types of work. Steeplejacks need it and so do surgeons. Square Knotting is a craft in itself for weaving cord into all sorts of things from belts and handbags to tablecloths.

Sometimes the Square Knot also is used for knotting together two pieces of string or small cord of the same size. But there are more secure knots for tying the ends of two ropes together, especially if they are large or of different sizes or stiffness.

One of the advantages of a Square Knot, when properly used as a Binder Knot, is that it may be slipped apart by giving it a simple tug at either end of the knot. But this can be dangerous when large ropes are tied together with it because the knot easily may become fouled and pull apart by itself. Serious accidents have been known to happen. If there is any question of safety, a Bend should be used to tie ropes together rather than a Square Knot.

A Square Knot is tied by passing the left end *over* and *under* the right end and then by crossing what is now the right end *over* and *under* the left. The two ends should leave each loop lying side by side.

If you make a mistake and the ends come out on opposite sides of each loop, with one end under and one over, the result will be the weak *Granny Knot* (Plate Number 1), which should never be tied on purpose for any practical use. *To upset a Square Knot,* simply pull either of the ends straight out away from the knot. It then may be slipped free, which is the easiest way of untying it.

The *Surgeon's Knot,* which surgeons sometimes use in operations but seldom call by that name, also is a practical one for tying packages and binding together many small things with light cord or twine. Sometimes known as the *Ligature Knot,* it keeps the first tie from slipping before the knot is completed. It is made the same way as a Square Knot, but with an extra turn of the left end over and under during the first part of the tie (see Plate Number 1), and then is finished off just as a Square Knot would be.

A *Bowknot,* used for tying shoestrings, ribbons and packages, is another close relative of the Square Knot, except that the second half-knot is tied with two bights rather than two ends. Many of the knots called *Parcel Knots* start with a Bowknot and are then finished off with extra twists of the bights or ends. A good Parcel Knot can be tied by starting with a regular Bowknot and putting the right bight through the left bight. A pull on the right end will draw the knot down tight.

The *Thief Knot,* which looks so much like a Square Knot it is hard to tell them apart, is tied in an entirely different way. It was the legendary crime detector knot of the high seas. A Thief Knot puts the standing parts of the two ends of rope on opposite sides of the knot, instead of both on the same side as in a Square Knot.

When a sailor suspected somebody of stealing valuables from his sea bag, he tied the bag with a Thief Knot instead of a Square Knot and then left the suspected thief alone with it. If the thief opened the bag to steal something and retied it with the usual Square Knot, the owner could tell immediately that he had been robbed. The Thief Knot also is known as a *Bread Knot* because cooks aboard the old sailing vessels used it to find out who was raiding the kitchen bread bag for snacks to eat.

Unlike the Square Knot, it is not formed by making two half knots. To tie a Thief Knot (Plate Number 1), take the rope in the left hand and form a bight by bending the end in toward yourself. Hold this horizontally, the bight toward the right.

Take the other end of the rope and thread it from beneath up through the bight. Now bring this same end out toward yourself and then down around and under both sides of the bight. Cross it over the top of the far side of the bight and pull it down and through. It should look exactly like a Square Knot, but with the standing parts opposite.

Loop Knots

Loop Knots usually are used to fasten a rope to something. They generally are tied in the hand and then put over the object to which they are fastened, which is the difference between them and hitches made directly around an object. When tied properly and drawn tight, Loop Knots give good security. They may be tied either in the bight or in the middle of a rope and will hold their shape so that the same knot may be used many times.

The *Bowline* probably is the most popular of the Loop Knots, because it can be used to serve many jobs well. Carefully formed and tightened, it will not slip or jam and yet may be untied easily. The Bowline may be thrown over a post for mooring a boat, tied in the end of a rope for hoisting, used for tying leaders of fishing lines, attaching a water ski rope, or the ropes of a backyard swing. With a rope the proper strength, the Bowline lowers and lifts men at work.

It takes its name from a ship's line called the *bow line,* once used to trim a square sail during the old seafaring days. Captain John Smith praised the knot as being so firm that when it was "fastened by the bridles into the creengles of the sailes, they will breake, or the saile split before it will slip."

The Bowline (Plate Number 2) may be tied by first grasping the standing part of the rope so it comes through the palm of the left hand and drawing the end two or three feet to the right. Drop the end of the rope. With the right hand, form a small overhand loop against the palm of the left hand. Now bring the end up from beneath through this loop. Pass the end around behind and under the standing part of the rope and bring it back down through the same first loop. Both the end and the loop should be drawn tight.

An *Overhand Loop* (Plate Number 2), simply tied by doubling the rope and making an Overhand Knot in it, makes a useful knot when it is necessary to fasten a rope in the middle and leave both ends free for other work, as when lashing a truck load or a tarpaulin. This is an easy Loop Knot that has many uses around home, shop or farm. It also is a quick loop fastening for a peg or a hook. But it does jam under strain and sometimes is hard to untie.

The *Honda Knot* (Plate Number 2), also called the *Bowstring Knot*, has been known for years by primitive peoples in many parts of the world. It is one of the oldest of knots, long used by the archers of ancient Europe, as well as by the Indians of North America, to secure their bowstrings. Perhaps the Mexican cattlemen learned it from the Indians and passed the knowledge along to the cowhands of the West who used it to make a loop for their lariats. The Honda Knot makes the smallest and most open of the Loop Knots.

It is easily made by tying a loose Overhand Knot about a foot from the end of the rope and passing the end part way through it from the opposite side. Tie another small Overhand Knot in the end for a stopper and draw it tight. Instead of tying a Stopper Knot in the end, it may be seized (whipped to the standing part) with yarn.

To make a lariat, the other end of the rope is put through the Honda Knot. When it is used as a lariat, instead of merely as a Loop Knot in one end to fasten the rope to something, it becomes a Noose.

A *Lineman's Loop* is strong and safe, holds equally well with a pull from either direction and forms and loosens easily. It generally is considered among the best and most practical of Loop Knots whenever it is necessary to make loops in the standing part of a rope.

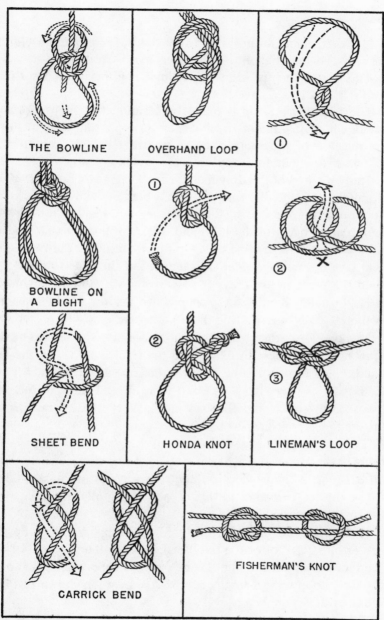

THE BOWLINE

OVERHAND LOOP

①

BOWLINE ON A BIGHT

①

②

×

SHEET BEND

②

HONDA KNOT

③

LINEMAN'S LOOP

CARRICK BEND

FISHERMAN'S KNOT

PLATE № 2

It is used for hand-holds and foot-holds, for mountain climbing and as a man harness. Utility linemen often depend on it for mounting poles to fix wires. Sometimes it also is called a *Lineman's Rider.*

The Lineman's Loop is made by forming two loops, folding one down against the other, and then a simple pull-through. But the twisting of the loops may be puzzling unless each step is followed slowly and exactly until the knack is learned.

Study the first of the drawings for the Lineman's Loop in Plate Number 2. Double the rope to form a bight. Make an Overhand Loop, crossing the end to the left as shown. Hold that with the thumb and fingers of the left hand. Next form a smaller Underhand Loop below the first one. Do this by bringing the same end you have been using *under* the other leg of the rope to the right. Hold the place where these cross with the thumb and fingers of the right hand. Bend the top loop down against the bottom one as though you were shutting the lid to a box.

The two loops together should now look like the second of the drawings. Hold these in place with the right hand. With the left hand, reach from behind and grasp the rope at the point marked X. Bend this away from you and then up and through the two loops. Draw on it and the two ends. Work the knot with the fingers to shape it properly.

The most useful of the *Double Loop Knots* for attaching something to the center of a rope when the ends are tied is the *Bowline on a Bight.* This provides parallel loops which may be used to lift an injured person or to sling a ladder as a platform for painting or other work.

A Bowline on a Bight may be started by doubling up the center of a rope to form a double bight. Pass the very end of the loop up through this bight. Then draw this loop back down over the large loop until it finally reaches the position shown in Plate Number 2.

When using it to rescue an injured person, one of his legs is put through each loop and he holds to the double standing part with his hands. If he is unconscious, a single hitch from the standing part is put around his chest and under his arms.

The *Noose* is a different kind of a Loop Knot in that it doesn't hold its shape. Its purpose is to slip and tighten around something as when the Honda Knot is formed into a Noose in making a lariat. The Noose is any knot at the end of a rope that tightens when the rope is pulled.

A *Simple Noose* is what most of us know as the common *Slip Knot*, which is made by tying an Overhand Knot and pulling a bight instead of a single end up through it. It is used on small rope and twine, especially for lashing packages, and its greatest advantage is the ease of tying it. However, it also jams easily, and a *Figure Eight Noose*, made by tying a Figure Eight Knot and passing the other end of the rope through it, draws up more smoothly.

A Noose that is made with a Bowline Knot, by tying the Bowline around a loop of its own standing part, is called the *Running Bowline Knot*. Almost any Loop Knot can be made into a Noose by pulling the bight of the rope a short distance through the loop.

Nooses are used for fastenings to posts and rings, sometimes in place of a hitch, as well as for lashings, and probably are among the first of all knots that were used by prehistoric man to snare animals for food. African natives, the bushmen of Australia, American Indians, hunters and poachers all made snares with some form of the Noose.

Snaring birds and small animals was a popular sport up until around the 1800's. Books for sportsmen in those days devoted many pages to the making of snares to trap larks, partridge and other birds with fine nooses of horsehair suspended between trees so the birds would fly into them at dusk and be caught. Rabbits, wolves and even mice were fair game for snaring. But the sport gradually lost popularity among civilized people when it became frowned on as being cruel to animals.

Bends for Joining Ropes

A *Bend* is used to tie two ropes together or to tie two ends of the same rope. Splices, of course, are stronger than any knot and should be used if ropes are to be joined permanently. Some bends are intended for smaller cord and twine and some are for larger rope. When ropes are tied to each other, they should be the same size and material.

The *Sheet Bend* (Plate Number 2) serves most general needs for tying small or medium size ropes together. It takes its name from its use aboard sailing vessels where it was trimmed to the lower corner of a sail and also is known as a *Common Bend* or *Simple Bend.* It is secure, unties easily, and doesn't damage rope.

Make an Overhand Loop with one end as shown in the illustration. Bring the other rope end up through the loop, around behind the standing part, and back down through the loop. Draw all the parts tight.

The *Carrick Bend,* while somewhat bulky, is one of the strongest of knots. It is easy to untie, nearly slip-proof, and seldom jams even when watersoaked. It is the bend commonly tied in heavy rope and cables and has many decorative as well as practical uses because of its symmetrical appearance.

Follow the illustrations in Plate Number 2 to tie it. Take one end of rope and make an Underhand Loop in such a way that the free end and standing part both point away from you. Rest this loop across the other end of rope as shown. This end should lie beneath both sides of the loop.

Now cross the second rope end *over* the standing part of the first rope and *under* the free end of the first rope. Bring it around *over* the left side of the loop. Cross it *under* itself and out *over* the right side of the loop. Draw it up as tightly as possible. It may be finished off by seizing the ends to their own standing parts with yarn or twine.

There are a number of different Fishing Knots that are used as bends. A good one to join lengths of twine together, as when adding an extra piece to tie a package, is the *Fisherman's Knot* shown in Plate Number 2. Simply lap the two ends and tie an Overhand Knot in each around the standing part of the other. Pull the knots tight and draw them together.

Hitches and Other Fastenings

Hitches generally are tied around something instead of being tied in the hand. They are quick and temporary ways of fastening rope and usually can be released as quickly. Some untie themselves by falling apart when whatever they are hitched around is removed.

It sometimes is said that with a few basic hitches, the average person can take care of nearly all his temporary tying needs. While there are other knots that are better for specific jobs with rope, hitches are reliable, handy and simple to use.

Hitches are used for clotheslines and life lines, to tie around garden stakes or over posts to hold back crowds at fires or during street repair excavations. They are needed to lash trunks, bales and bundles as well as truck cargoes. Hitches help rope to haul, tow and lift, to moor ships and tether horses, and to work blocks and tackle and slings.

The word "hitch" is an old one, but according to legend it took its meaning when applied to knots of this kind from the men of the early whaling ships who used to form a Clove Hitch to fasten a hemp whale line to the shank of a harpoon. However, sailors were using hitches, by whatever names they called them, long before whalers came on the scene. Men in at least fifty types of work other than sailing, from farmers to stevedores, would find it hard to do their daily jobs without a knowledge of hitches.

A good way to practice the forming of hitches is around a cardboard mailing tube or short length of thick wooden rod. For fastenings around things with square edges, a piece of two-by-four makes a fine practice block.

A *Half Hitch* is made simply by passing one end of the rope around an object and then passing the end under the rope, as if tying a common Overhand Knot. It is drawn tight against the object by pulling the standing part. Used this way, as shown in the illustration in Plate Number 3, it is *not* a reliable fastening. However, this is the first step in making many other hitches.

A more secure way of using the Half Hitch by itself, if the pull against it is steady, is shown in the second drawing. The end has been nipped at the top turn of the rope away from the standing part. As long as it isn't loosened or shaken, this will serve well for temporary use and is a very quick fastening.

The third drawing shows a *Slipped Half Hitch.* Notice that the end crosses *under* the pulled-out loop and that the nip, or point of pressure, is still well above the standing part. An easy pull on the end releases the hitch. Artists sometimes use a cord fastened with a Slipped Half Hitch for carrying their canvases. Tied around a tree branch, it often is used by mountain climbers to hold fast the end of a rope for lowering equipment to a level below. Small boat lines may be hitched to spars with it.

If whatever the rope is tied around is of small diameter, a *Figure Eight Hitch,* as illustrated, may be better.

Two Half Hitches, as the name suggests, is a hitch made by tying the Half Hitch twice. Although it is easily tied merely by bringing the end around twice, there also is a trick way of doing it. Put the rope around the object and tie it with a Granny Knot. Now pull away from it with the standing part of the rope and it will capsize into Two Half Hitches.

Ships frequently are moored with Two Half Hitches. It is a hitch the archer uses to finish tying off his bowstring after he has secured it to the lower end of the bow with a Clove Hitch. In fruit warehouses, cords with Two Half Hitches hold bunches of bananas that are strung from ceiling hooks. Sailors use Two Half Hitches in rigging lines, hunters for hanging large game from tree limbs, stevedores to hoist barrels and upholsterers in making mattress tufts.

An auto tow rope may be fastened by taking a Round Turn with the rope before making Two Half Hitches. If it is hitched to

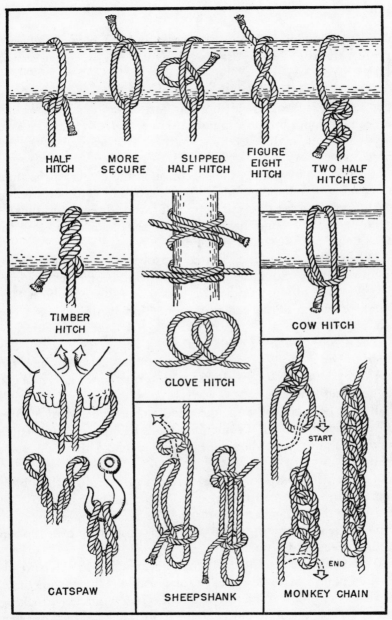

HALF HITCH

MORE SECURE

SLIPPED HALF HITCH

FIGURE EIGHT HITCH

TWO HALF HITCHES

TIMBER HITCH

CLOVE HITCH

COW HITCH

CATSPAW

SHEEPSHANK

MONKEY CHAIN

START

END

PLATE Nº 3

a bumper, padding should be put around the bumper edges to protect the rope before drawing it tight. Otherwise, the strands may break.

The *Timber Hitch* as shown in the illustration, Plate Number 3, is a practical one for hoisting logs, bales, small crates, and especially things that are round in shape. It doesn't jam and can be freed quickly, almost falling apart by itself as soon as the pull is released.

It is started by putting the rope around the center of the thing to be hoisted and making a Half Hitch around the rope's standing part. Then turn the rope back on itself two or three times, tucking it around in the same direction as the lay of the rope. Pull the ends under and work the knot tight.

When the Timber Hitch is used for towing something or hoisting it on end, it should be formed below the center of the object and the rope brought up a little and then fastened with a Half Hitch or two near the end in the direction in which it is to be hauled.

The *Clove Hitch* (Plate Number 3) comes as close as any hitch to being an all-purpose tie. It is not as secure as some, but it does well enough for an almost endless number of uses and can be tied readily in a variety of ways.

It may be made either in the middle or at the end of a rope. When used at the end, it sometimes tends to slip, so a Half Hitch to the standing part should be added to make the hold more secure.

To hitch the end of the rope, make a turn around the object and then lead the rope up *over* itself and around a second time and bring the end under the crossing. *To hitch the middle of the rope,* make two opposite loops as shown, drop them over the top of the object, and draw tight.

Carpenters use the Clove Hitch, with the turns loosely spread, to sling planks of wood on edge for hoisting. Millers sometimes tied sacks of grain with a *Slipped Clove Hitch,* made by tucking the end back under to form a slip loop, for easy release from around the neck of the sack. Netmakers generally fasten the first tier of meshes to the headline of a net with Clove Hitches. It is sometimes called the *Builder's Knot* because it was so widely used to hitch staging to upright posts.

The *Cow Hitch* (Plate Number 3) has many names and relatives. It is used by the farmer to hitch a cow's tether to a post or bar. In horse and buggy days, it frequently held the carriage reins to the hitching post. The sailor, who sometimes called it a *Lanyard Hitch*, used it for fastening a small lanyard line to the large shroud rigging that supported the mast. Tied in the bight of a continuous loop of rope or endless strap to be slung around a bale or barrel for hoisting, it is known as a *Bale Sling Hitch*.

When the same basic hitch is used for decorative rope work it takes the name of a *Lark's Head*. Tied with an Eye Splice, it becomes a *Running Eye*. Used to hitch a hoisting sling or double rope to a metal ring, it is called a *Ring Hitch*. But most of us probably know it best as a *Tag Knot* because it is the usual way of fastening a string to a price tag.

Despite all its names and uses, the Cow Hitch is one of the easiest hitches to tie and also one of the least likely to come untied by accident. Just double a rope near one end or at the center, depending on how you intend to use it, and put both thicknesses around what it is to be tied to. Reach *through* the loop and bring *back* through it both the end and the standing part.

The *Catspaw* is the hitch nearly always used for attaching a rope sling to a hook to lift heavy loads. It doesn't slip or jam, but it falls apart instantly when the hook is removed. It has done a good job of lifting heavy things since at least the 1770's and still is considered the most practical of all *Hook Hitches*.

It is tied by taking a bight of the rope in each hand and holding them well apart and then twisting the rope three full turns, away from you, with both hands. This should produce the form illustrated in Plate Number 3. Bring the two loops together and put them over the bill of the hook.

The *Sheepshank* is the best method for temporarily shortening a rope by gathering in unnecessary slack. If the rope is large, the slack is laid on the floor or ground in parallel lengths. With smaller rope, the slack may be gathered the same way in the hand. Then make a loop in the standing part of one end to form a Half Hitch and put it over the bight of the slack rope, drawing the Half Hitch tight as it is made. Do the same with the other end. The result should be as shown in Plate Number 3. To make it more secure, the end of each loop may be seized or tied with several turns to the standing part next to it.

Sometimes a Sheepshank is used to protect a weak section of rope by taking some of the strain off it until it can be replaced. When the Sheepshank is used for this, the weak section should be in the center length of the gathered slack.

Another way of shortening string and small cord is with the **Monkey Chain** (Plate Number 3), which is nothing more than the familiar chain stitch borrowed from crocheting. The Monkey Chain often is used around the house for shortening such things as window drape cords and electric light pulls in an attractive way. Because of its many sharp bends, it is a poor shortening for rope of larger size.

Start it by tying a loose Slip Knot. Bend the loop down to the standing part of the cord. Reach through the loop of the knot and pull up a bight of cord. Continue in the same way until you have formed as many "links" of the chain as you wish. Finish off the Monkey Chain by putting the end through the last loop.

The Monkey Chain also has an emergency use. If you need a rope heavier than you have available, a small cord can be made into a temporarily thicker "rope" by forming a large-looped chain with it. However, not too much trust should be placed in its strength.

Two Simple Splices

Splicing is the strongest way to join two ropes, to make a sling or endless rope for hoisting, or to form a permanent eye loop in the end of one rope. While a knot may cut the strength of a rope in half, a good splice has more than nine-tenths the strength of the rope itself.

Actually, splicing is a form of weaving. Some splices require expert skill, but simple splicing is not difficult. It often looks harder to the beginner than it really is. Care and patience are needed more than any special talent.

Ropes must be the same size to be spliced and should be tightly twisted and in good condition. Braided cord or rope cannot be spliced. Some synthetic fiber ropes are harder to splice than those of natural fiber. They usually should have the ends of their strands wound with adhesive tape during splicing to prevent unraveling. The strands of natural fiber ropes more than an inch in diameter also should be whipped or bound with tape, but that isn't necessary for smaller rope.

There are many types of splicing, but the *Short Splice* will serve most ordinary needs for joining two ropes. Although it does thicken the rope so that it can't be used through pulleys, it is the strongest of splices and the easiest to make.

Follow the illustrations of Plate Number 4. Take your time and keep the splice even. If two strands happen to go under one strand, remove them and reweave correctly. Keep twisting each strand tight as the splice is made. A small pair of duck-billed pliers may be of help in splicing. Do your splicing at a bench or table where there is a comfortable place to sit.

To Make the Short Splice: 1. Untwist each rope end a short distance. If the ropes are large, whip the ends at the point to which they have been unlayed. Put the two ends together as closely as possible so that each strand of one rope lies between two strands of the other as shown. Now draw the strands of the first end along the second end of rope and hold them with one hand, or tie them there temporarily if the rope is a big one.

2. Moving across the twist of the rope, take any one strand end over the neighboring strand and thread it under the next strand. Take another strand end and repeat the over and under weave with it. Take the remaining strand end and repeat the

weave again. Give each of these separate strands a twist to keep the yarns together and gently draw them up tight. Check to make sure the strands come out at even spaces around the rope.

3. Turn the rope end for end or move around to the other side of the bench. Weave the strand ends of the second rope into the strands of the first in exactly the same way, tucking each strand over and under those that lay alongside. Now go back to the first end again and do the same with that.

4. Repeat the weaving on both ropes at least two times for each strand end to complete the splicing.

5. Cut off each strand, but don't cut too close. Leave short ends outside the rope so as to allow for the strands pulling back into it under wear and tension when the rope is put to work. Roll the splice on a smooth surface to set it.

An *Eye Splice* is made to form a permanent loop at the end of a rope. Sometimes it is spliced right through a metal ring or other fastening, but it also may be a free loop for dropping over a post or hook or to serve as a hand-hold. See Plate Number 4.

The sailor uses a small pointed stick called a "fid," in making an Eye Splice. A good home substitute is an orangewood stick, such as is used for manicuring the fingernails, or a thin pencil that is pointed but has the lead broken off. Even a large blunt nail will do. The weaving is much the same as with the Short Splice, each end strand being tucked first under one strand of the rope and then over the next.

Start the Eye Splice by placing the rope on the bench so the end points toward you. Bend the end of the rope up to the right to form an eye of the wanted size. Untwist the end six or seven turns. Spread the three strands away from you fanwise. See A, Plate Number 4. Put the end strands against the standing part of the rope where it is to be entered.

Now untwist the rope itself one half turn. Push the stick under the top or center strand of the twisted open rope. Take the center strand of the end and thread it under the center strand of the rope from right to left. Next tuck the left strand of the end under

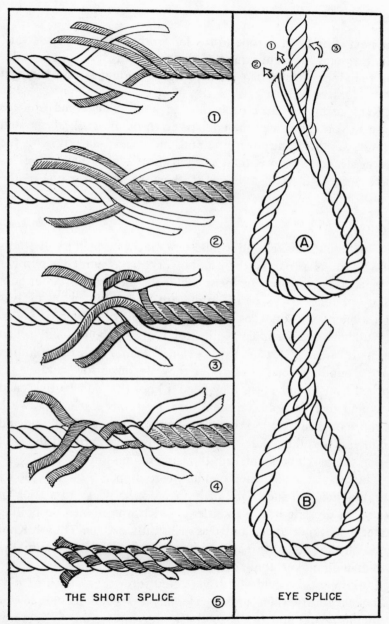

THE SHORT SPLICE ① ② ③ ④ ⑤

EYE SPLICE Ⓐ Ⓑ

PLATE № 4

the next strand of the rope to the left in the same direction. Last of all, thread the right strand of the end from right to left under the remaining strand of rope. The result should be as shown in Plate Number 4, B.

Keep using the stick each time to hold each strand of rope open so you can thread the end strand through. Tuck all the end strands another time, over one and under one, starting with the center strand as before, then left and then right. Finally, to complete the job, trim off the ends so they are about as long as the rope is thick.

Knots on the Job

The butcher, baker and candlestick maker, as well as all others who tie knots as part of their daily work, have learned a number of special ways of using them that help them do a better job. Many of these tricks of the trade are interesting in themselves and some may be of occasional use to the rest of us who tie knots.

Butchers use a simple Noose for tying up boned and rolled roasts of meat. They draw it tight and Half Hitch the standing part around the end. But when they tie meat for pickling, as corned beef or salt pork, they need a knot that can be tightened now and then to hold the meat together firmly during the week or more of shrinking. So they tie a Square Knot and pull one end to upset it and then Half Hitch the standing part around the end. When the pickling is finished, they add a final hitch.

The candlemaker, when candles were dipped by hand, used a simple Hitch to fasten each of a dozen or so wicks to a stick or board for dipping into the kettle in which wax floated on boiling water. The tailor and seamstress constantly use the Thumb Knot to tie off the ends of thread and it is the favorite of the sailmaker and awning maker, too.

Large knots of gold and silver often form the pattern of pins and rings the jeweler makes. He has a special technique for stringing pearls and beads. Usually, they are strung on several strands of silk or nylon, according to their size, with a knot after each bead or after each group of five or more. Each knot is tied by putting the beads through the loop rather than by pulling the free ends of the cords through it. At the end of the string of beads, the cord is brought back through the last bead and knotted, then threaded back out again to fasten it to the clasp.

The weaver uses a different knot for almost each type of cloth, many similar to the Sheet Bend or Square Knot, and they have to be tied rapidly so as not to stop the loom. A series of Figure Eight Knots are what the rush seat maker uses as he hand-twists his reeds. The quilter ties off his ends of strong twine with a Square Knot.

Carpenters find the Timber Hitch convenient for hoisting boards. When a carpenter asks his helper to hitch a hammer to a rope so he can pull it up to where he is working, the line is always fastened around the head of the hammer, not the handle, to keep it from slipping in midair to fall on somebody. Usually a Slip Knot is drawn up between the claws and then a hitch taken around the peen of the hammer.

The lineman hauls his wire up to the arm of a utility pole with a *Bell Ringer's Knot,* which is merely the first half of a Sheepshank. He passes a loop around the hank of wire and Half Hitches it to the standing part. When the church bell ringer tied the knot, it was to keep the long end of bell rope from dragging on the belfry floor while it wasn't in use.

A surgeon has to be a careful knot-maker because if he ties a poor knot in taking his stitches during an operation it may slip and cause internal troubles or more of a scar than necessary. While some surgeons use the Surgeon's Knot, others feel it is too big and prefer the simple Square Knot. Sometimes the knot is tied by holding the ends with two pairs of scissors.

Bandages usually are fastened with adhesive tape, but in an emergency a bandage may be torn down the middle a few inches, after it has been wrapped around an arm or finger, and then half knotted at the ends. These are passed around and tied together with a Square Knot, being careful that it isn't so tight it will stop circulation.

A violinist or guitarist often knots the strings of his instrument with a Figure Eight Knot, doubling the end before tying, if need be.

The mechanical binder used by the farmer is partly a knot-tying machine. It ties a knot that a man can't tie by hand well enough to use, an Overhand Bend with the bights tucked instead of the ends. But the farmer may use a method even more ancient than a block and tackle to lower a cut log from a tree. He simply winds his lowering rope around a stout branch with a single Round Turn. This will let him lower something several times his own weight, but is no good for hoisting.

A gardener who wants to support a young plant by tying it to a stick or trellis avoids the bother of trying to hold the two together and adjust them while making a knot. He doubles his cord, puts it around both stem and support, gives it an easy Ring Hitch and then draws it as taut as he wishes and ties a final knot without having to hold all the rest in position while he is doing it.

The sailor, of course, gave us most of our knots as well as most of the names for them. Sailing ships depended as much on rope and knots as on sails and the men aboard had to know more about them than anybody else, so they invented at least ten times as many knots as workers at any other trade. Knotting probably reached its peak as an art and craft, as well as a need of work, during the early 1800's.

In those days, boys often went to sea before the age of ten and many sailors never learned to read or write, so they had nothing much to occupy their idle hours. But there was always rope around and a sailor could busy his hands with that. Knots often became his hobby. Sailors made a constant game of tying knots, competing with each other and priding themselves in the tricks they learned that no landlubber could perform. Fancy knots decorated nearly everything they made or owned.

The sailor's term for all the different kinds of rope work he does, caring for rope and handling it as well as knotting and splicing, is *marlinespike seamanship*. A "marlinespike" was a pointed iron pin used to splice rope. Today, as in the past, marlinespike seamanship usually comes first in a sailor's learning. Sails or none, knots are still vital to the man of the sea.

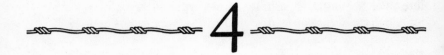

4

Tricky Knots and Puzzles

EVERYWHERE that there is rope or string, people have found ways to have fun with it. Sailors, lumbermen, cowhands, Indians, African natives and South Sea islanders all have their favorite trick knots and puzzles.

Scientists who have gone to remote parts of the world to make their studies of mankind often have found primitive people doing many of the same stunts with knots that the New England sailor considered his own. Tying knots for fun is a universal pastime. Rope is inexpensive, easy to carry around, and a trick or puzzle once learned is a lifetime bit of amusement, both for the one who can do it and for all those who will watch and wish they knew how.

While any kind of small rope, string, or even a large handkerchief twisted ropewise by its diagonal corners can be used for fun with knots, the best to use is a five-foot length of soft unglazed hollow-braided cotton cord. Manila rope is rather stiff and tends to twist and kink. When string is needed, as it is for some of the puzzles, it should be soft white cotton. Nylon and most synthetics are too slippery.

Tricky Ways to Tie Knots

A speedy method of tying an Overhand Knot in midair is one that sailors sometimes called a *Lightning Knot* (Plate Number 5). An old salt, showing off his skill, might be heard to boast that it is the "fastest knot in the world."

Hold the left hand with the thumb up and the palm facing you, fingertips to the right. Drape one end of the rope over the hand so that the end hangs down over the *back* of it. Now take the other end of the rope in the right hand, but in the opposite way, so the end goes across the *palm* of it. The right hand should have the thumb toward the ceiling, palm facing you, and fingertips pointed to the left.

Show the hands apart with the rope hanging between them. Bring the hands together so the left hand is nearer your body, with the backs of the left fingertips touching against the palm of the right hand. Tightly nip the *right* end of rope between the *left* first and second fingers. At the same time, nip the *left* end of rope between the *right* first and second fingers. Merely pull the hands straight apart and an Overhand Knot will form in the center of the rope.

Learn to do it slowly and then practice until you can seem to pick up the rope casually and form the instant knot just by a swift passing of the hands. There are several variations of the Lightning Knot. They may be shown as part of a puzzling routine to follow the first one.

For a *Shoulder Knot,* hold one end of the rope with the left hand so the end hangs down across the palm as the hand is held straight out from you. Drop the other end of the rope on the left shoulder and leave it there.

With the free right hand, reach toward the left, between the bottom of the left arm and the hanging rope. At the same time, bring the left hand over to touch the right shoulder so as to cross your arms in front of you. With the right hand, take the end of rope that has been hanging on your left shoulder. Keeping hold of the ends, slowly spread your arms wide apart and a knot will form in the rope between them.

You can make an *Arm Knot* in almost the same way. Hold one end of rope so it hangs down over the back of the left hand. Toss the other end across the held out left arm. It should hang over the arm, in a direction away from you, about midway between the wrist and elbow.

Reach with the free right hand toward the left through the loop. Grasp the end of rope hanging across the arm and pull it to the right. At the same time, dip the left arm slightly towards the floor to let the forming knot fall over the hand to the middle of the rope. This should all be done as one smooth continuous movement. Don't jerk on the end of the rope, but draw it out easily.

You may want to show a *Wrist Loop* next. Take one end in each hand, palms up and the rope hanging in front of you. Bring both palms up toward yourself. The right hand should be closer to your body than the left. Pass the right hand out over the top of your left wrist and down behind it, until the right hand is a foot or two nearer the floor than the left.

With the right hand that is still holding its own end of the rope, reach through the loop hanging across the left wrist. Pull down against it and toward the right with the back of the right wrist. The loop will fall over the right wrist and tighten around it. Now drop *both* ends of rope and it will be left tied there around the right wrist.

The sailor's favorite trick knot probably was the *Tom Fool's Knot,* which closely resembles an ordinary Bowknot except for the final crossing of the ends as they leave the bow (see Plate Number 5). Its practical use was to form temporary rope handcuffs, one loop being slipped over each of the prisoner's wrists. When using it as a stunt, the sailor made a quick knot of it, with much wiggling of the fingers to confuse the watcher.

Once the knack has been learned, it can be made in far less time than it takes to read how it is done. Hold up the right hand,

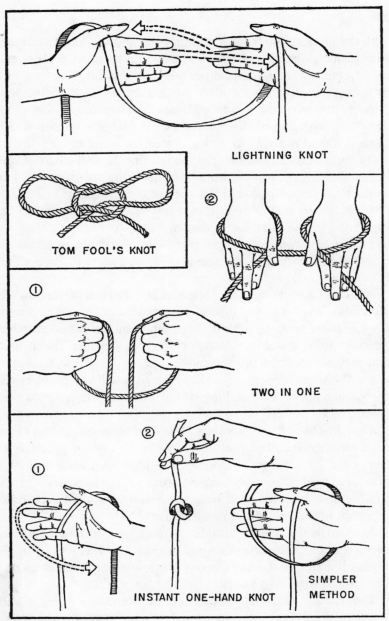

LIGHTNING KNOT

TOM FOOL'S KNOT

② ①

TWO IN ONE

① ②

INSTANT ONE-HAND KNOT

SIMPLER
METHOD

PLATE N⁰ 5

with the palm to the front, the thumb up and the fingers pointing toward the right. Drape the rope over the hand so a short end, about one foot long, hangs down across the palm. The long end, or rest of the rope, should hang down over the back of the hand.

Bring the left hand down, with the thumb pointing *down,* and grasp the long end of the rope. Close the fingers around it in a loose upside-down fist. Bring the closed left hand toward the left and turn it thumb up. Open out the left fingers so the end of rope lies behind them. Now turn the right hand inward from the wrist so the right fingertips touch the back of the left hand.

With the *right* first and second fingers, grasp the end of the rope lying across the back of the *left* hand. At the same time, the *left* first and second fingers grasp the end of rope lying across the *right* palm. Slowly draw the hands apart and you will have a Tom Fool's Knot.

An easy way to make a *Speedy Bowknot* is to follow the directions given for the first of the tricky knots, the Lightning Knot, except to start off with the hands much closer together. There should be only about a foot of rope between them. Start that way and then make the moves exactly as in the Lightning Knot. With less rope in the middle, the ends will catch up instead of passing through, resulting in a Bowknot rather than an Overhand.

Two In One (Plate Number 5) is a stunt in which two Overhand Knots are tied at the same time in a single rope. Start by laying the rope across the outstretched palms with a little less than a foot of each end hanging from the thumb sides of the hands. Close both fists and twist the hands in toward each other as shown in the first of the illustrations.

Now open the fingers straight out and grasp the two ends between the first and second fingers of each hand as shown in the second illustration. Gently shake the loops over the hands so they slip off and form two knots.

The *Instant One-Hand Knot* (Plate Number 5) starts with placing the rope over the right hand, thumb toward yourself and fingers pointing at upward angle to the right as illustrated. The end hanging over the back of the hand should be less than a foot long. Grip the longer end, which crosses the palm, between the third and little fingers. Now bend the hand straight down from the wrist, with fingertips toward the floor, and back under to nip the short end between the first and second fingers. Shake the loop down over the hand.

A simpler way, but a little less impressive, is to use both hands to put the rope into position for shaking off the knot. Start by placing the rope across the right hand as above. Then with the left hand, openly bring the short end up to the fingertips of the right hand as shown in the drawing. A quick forward and downward shake of the hand will produce the instant knot.

The *One-Handed Ring Hitch* (Plate Number 6) looks very tricky when made with a quick flourish. Hold the right hand palm down, fingers pointing to the right, thumb toward the person watching. Hang the center of the rope over the outthrust thumb. Keep the thumb pointing out as it is and bend the fingers down toward yourself until their tips point to the floor. Grasp the side of rope that is nearest you between the first and second fingers.

Now, still keeping the thumb pointed out as it has been, raise the fingers up flat again, tips pointing to the right, as they were when you started. But as you do so tilt them slightly to the front so the rope clipped between the first and second fingers will fall naturally across the back of the first finger at its tip. The position now should be that it passes up between the first and second fingers and hangs down over the left side of the first finger.

Turn the hand so the palm faces front and touch the tip of the first finger to the tip of the thumb. Let the loop that is on the finger slide over to the thumb to join the other loop and the hitch has been formed. When you learn to do it properly, the whole thing will look like one quick flip of the fingers, down and back.

In addition to being a standard hitch, it allows for some amusing by-play. Hold it at its base and lift it to one eye and it appears to be a comic monocle. Open it out wide and hold it to both eyes and the loops look like a funny pair of glasses.

A *Sheepshank* also may be tied in a trick way. Both this and the quick Ring Hitch makes more of an impression on people who have tied these knots in their regular form than on those who don't know what they should look like when finished. But they are interesting to show any group.

The fancy way of making this Sheepshank is with the loops illustrated in Plate Number 6. Hold the left hand in front of you, thumb up and fingers pointing right. Drape the rope over the hand so that most of it hangs down behind the hand and a short end hangs across the palm. With the right hand, grasp the long end of rope about a foot below the hand. Bring it up to the left of the short end. Now give it a twist to the left to form a loop and hang it over the fingers of the left hand.

Repeat the same twisting move and hang another loop on the left fingers. You now should have three loops as shown. Draw the center bights out through the right and left loops and then draw on the two ends of rope and the trick Sheepshank will take shape.

Any Number of Knots (Plate Number 6) can be made to appear in an almost magical way strung along a rope coiled for a moment between the hands and then drawn out again. This is a good climax for an impromptu display of trick knot-tying skill.

Your choice as to the number of knots you wish to make will decide the length of rope that should be used. With a long rope, you can run a string of knots out across the width of a whole room. Although usually a trick, this method has been used to tie quick Overhand Knots in a rope for emergency hand-holds. It sometimes is called the *Fire Escape Knot.*

The way you coil the rope causes the knots to form. Hold it across both outstretched palms, the short end passing under the left thumb and hanging about a foot down to the left of the hand. The rope also crosses under the right thumb, the right hand being held about a foot apart from the left.

As if you were simply taking slack to coil the rope, close the right fist around it and turn the fist over toward the left. The back of the right hand is now uppermost and the thumb points toward the left. Turning the hand has twisted a loop of rope across the

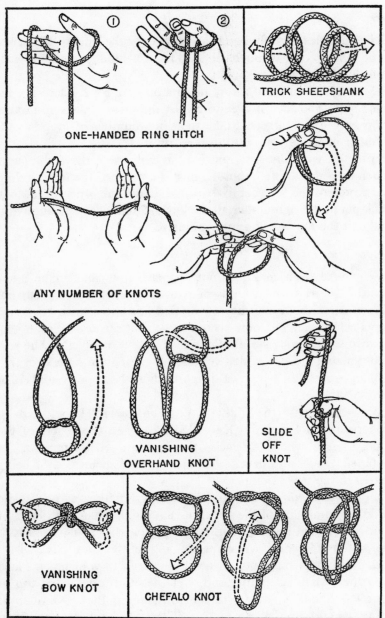

ONE-HANDED RING HITCH

TRICK SHEEPSHANK

ANY NUMBER OF KNOTS

VANISHING OVERHAND KNOT

SLIDE OFF KNOT

VANISHING BOW KNOT

CHEFALO KNOT

PLATE № 6

right knuckles. Simply hang this loop over the fingers of the left hand which come through the loop from behind, pointing toward you, to receive it.

Slide the right hand a foot or so along the rope. Close the fist once more and turn it over to repeat the move, hanging another loop on the left fingers. Make the same number of loops as the number of knots you wish to have appear.

Finally, with the first and second fingers of the right hand, reach in under all the loops, against the palm of the left hand, to the crotch of the left thumb. Nip that end of the rope and draw it back out to the right under all the loops. Shake the rope out by the end and the knots will appear along it.

Knots That Are Not

We have been making knots appear, now let's make some vanish. There are two kinds of vanishing knots. One group includes knots that really have been tied and these must be untied to vanish, either by some secret move that covers their untying or with a seemingly skillful flourish that does it openly. The second type are those in which you merely pretend to tie a knot that looks genuine but which falls apart when the rope is shaken or drawn out.

Let's start with the tricky ways to make real knots seem to disappear. An Overhand Knot tied loosely at the center of the rope, as it is when you make the Lightning Knot appear, for instance, may be vanished with a little flourish instead of being untied in the usual manner.

For a *Vanishing Overhand Knot,* begin with the knot in the middle and an end of the rope in each hand. Take both ends of rope in your left hand, holding them up together so the knot is at the bottom. Glance down at the crossings of the knot to see which end of the rope comes out of the knot nearest to your body. Place the rope that matches that end over the other one at the top in your left hand, as shown in the illustration, Plate Number 6. Bring the knot up towards you to the left hand and drop the loop of it over that end which is nearest you. Give the rope a gentle shake with the left hand and, as the loop drops down, the knot will fall out of it.

With a *Slide Off Knot* you can make it seem as though you slide a genuine Overhand Knot down a length of rope and right off the bottom. This, incidentally, is not a trick to try with manila rope or hard glazed sashcord as they are too rough on the hands. With a length of soft cotton rope, start by tying a fairly large and loose Overhand Knot about eight inches from one end. Hold the rope high by the other end with the left hand.

Now close the right hand around the knot in the form of a loose fist and, as you do so, secretly stick your thumb through the loop of the knot. This is the tricky move that should be hidden from those watching. Make it look casual, as though you simply were covering the big knot with your right hand. (See Plate Number 6.)

Just pull your right hand straight down and off the bottom of the rope and the knot will come free. Look in the mirror and you will see how effective it is. Practice until you can do it smoothly without hesitation. This is a stunt you safely may repeat several times without much chance that anyone will guess how it is done.

The *Vanishing Bowknot* is one that really is untied in plain view, but there is a little story to tell with it that makes watchers think you are making the knot tighter instead of undoing it, so that the vanish comes as a real surprise. Start by tying a large Bowknot in the center of the rope. If you wish, you may begin by making the Speedy Bowknot previously explained.

Say something to the effect that all of us know how handy a Bowknot is for tying packages or shoelaces since just a pull at the ends will untie it. Pull the ends and let it fall apart. Tie another Bowknot and hold it with both thumbs through the loops from the top so that both ends hang down free.

Point out that sometimes, by accident, the ends get tangled in the bows and then it gets into a real jam so it isn't easy to untie at all. Bring each of the ends up over the side of its neighboring bow and push it back *down through* from the top. Pull both ends and the knot will jam tightly. Untie the tangle with both hands.

Now tie a third Bowknot and explain that you have found a magic way to get around the trouble even when the ends become caught in the bows. Hold the loops with the thumbs pointing down through them from the top again. Lift the end to which your right thumb points *up through* the right bow and do the same with the left. (See the illustration, Plate Number 6.) Slowly pull the ends and the knot will look as if it were jamming tight again. But continue to pull and it will fall right apart, just as if the ends hadn't been put through the bows.

A whole *String of Vanishing Knots* may be shown by reversing the method of coiling the rope that was used to produce Any Number of Knots along it. Start by making the string of knots appear if you wish, or else merely by tying a series of Overhand Knots spaced out along a rope. They should be fairly large ones, tied in the normal manner so that the right-hand end of each knot comes out on the side of the rope nearest you.

Now lay the knot at the left end of the rope on the left palm and stack the next knot on top of it and so on. When all have been stacked, reach with the right hand down into the coil and pull the left end of the rope straight up through. Hold the other end of the rope with the left fingers, pull the hands apart slowly, and all the knots will vanish.

Any Square Knot becomes a *Vanishing Square Knot* by a simple move to cover the pull of the fingers in releasing it. To change a Square Knot into a Slip Knot, as already explained in the previous chapter, all you have to do is upset it by pulling one of the ends out from it at a right angle. Here's a way to do that secretly:

Tie two rope ends together with a Square Knot and show it. Hold your left hand with thumb up and fingers pointing right. Drop the tied rope over the left fingers so the knot falls into the palm of the hand. Remark that the knot should be real tight and give the upper end a little downward tug with your right fingers.

This makes a slip knot of it, but your covering hand conceals the fact from those watching.

Have someone take hold of the rope and pull. Clench your fist tightly and the knot will seem to hold. Make a pass over it and, as soon as you release the grip of your fingers, the end will pull free in the person's hands.

When you tie a *Chefalo Knot* (Plate Number 6), which takes its name from a famous Italian magician who invented it, you seem to be tying four knots into one tangled mass. But if the loopings shown in the illustration are followed, a pull at the ends lets them all fall free.

Start by tying a single knot in the center of the rope, but don't draw it tight. Tie another knot above it, as though you were tying the second half of a Square Knot. Notice in the illustration how the ends come out with the same sides towards you as in the first knot that was tied. Leave this second one loosely formed, too. Now bring the right end down through the lower knot as shown. Next bring the same end up around and out through the top knot. Slowly pull on the ends and it will all come untangled.

We come now to the second type of vanishing knots, in which no real knot is tied at all, but the tying of a genuine knot is pretended.

There are a number of ways of tying a *Fake Overhand Knot.* One convincing method starts with holding the end of the rope between the left thumb and middle joint of the first finger, palm facing you and fingertips pointing to the right. The short end of rope should hang over the back of the hand and the long end down the front.

Reach with the right hand to the center of the rope and bring it up to the left thumb and finger to form an Overhand Loop. Lightly hold the point where the top of the loop now crosses between the left thumb and finger. Take the right hand entirely away from it for a moment. The long end of rope should hang in front of the loop toward you as illustrated in Plate Number 7.

With the right hand, pick up the long end of the rope and put it out through the loop away from you. Pull the end on through as though you were really tying a knot. Draw the end down with the right hand, as if tightening the knot, which will pull the loop up into the left fingers.

As it reaches the left fingers, thrust the tip of your middle left finger toward yourself and push a small bight of rope into the tightening loop. Draw it up firmly and this will give you a slip knot which looks like a real Overhand Knot. A pull on the ends of rope makes the knot vanish.

A *Fake Square Knot* (Plate Number 7) is begun with an end of rope in each hand just as if you were going to tie a real Square Knot. But instead of tying the first part of a real knot by *crossing* the ends under and over, merely hold one end straight and twist the other end a full turn *around* it.

Then tie the second part of the knot exactly as you would tie the rest of a Square Knot by crossing the ends over and under. Pull them just as tight as you can. The fake knot looks very real and will hold itself in position until the rope is given a hard shake.

Rope and String Puzzles

Sailors who had to darn their own socks and sew buttons on their shirts themselves during the long months at sea when they were away from the women at home who might have performed those mending services for them had an amusing stunt with a piece of rope to show they could thread a needle "just as slick as any woman."

The Bachelor's Needle, as the trick is called, is among the oldest of rope puzzles. A length of cord with a knot at one end is wrapped several times around the left thumb and a small loop is made so it sticks up about an inch from between the thumb and first two fingers to represent the eye of the needle. The right hand picks up the knotted end and shoots forward with startling suddenness, seeming to thread it right through the loop faster than anyone could thread a needle.

If the wrapping around the thumb is done as shown in the

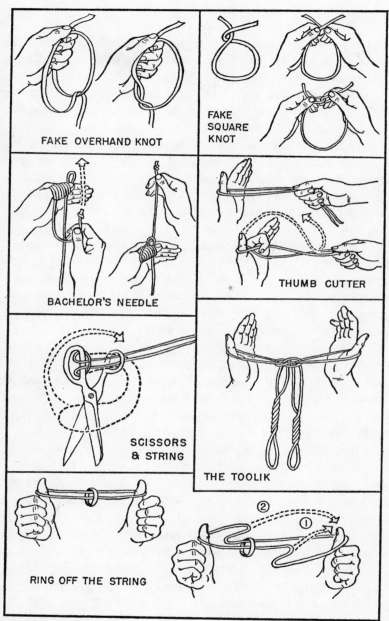

FAKE OVERHAND KNOT

FAKE SQUARE KNOT

BACHELOR'S NEEDLE

THUMB CUTTER

SCISSORS & STRING

THE TOOLIK

RING OFF THE STRING

PLATE № 7

illustration (Plate Number 7), the Bachelor's Needle works itself. Take a three-foot length of soft cotton cord or string and tie a small Stopper Knot in one end. With the left palm facing you and fingers pointed to the right, hang the knotted end over the left thumb. It should be toward the palm and should hang down a few inches beneath the hand.

Leave the knotted end where it is and wrap the cord around the thumb four times. Twist the cord back to make a one-inch loop and hold the loop between the end of the thumb and first two fingers. With the right hand, pick up the knotted end of the rope and pretend to thrust it forward suddenly through the small loop.

Actually, you pull the knotted end straight up and out toward the right, so it will come up between the thumb and fingers into the loop. It will do this by itself if pulled sharply in the right direction. Repeat the puzzle by drawing the knotted end back through the loop and pulling down the other end to make an even smaller eye of the needle for the second try.

The *Thumb Cutter* is a puzzle in which a cord doubly looped around the left thumb appears to pass right through it. Start by doubling the cord and hanging the center over the left thumb as illustrated in Plate Number 7. With the back of the hand toward those watching, secretly extend the left first finger across both strands and draw back the outer strand as shown.

Say that you will add another loop to make it twice as secure. Give the right hand, which is holding the two ends, a turn toward yourself so the strands cross in the manner illustrated. Bring the ends forward and put the thumb between the strands close to where your right hand holds them.

Pull the ends tight around the thumb. Have a watcher pull on the cord to convince himself that the hold is secure. Secretly slip the left fingertip out of its tiny loop. Ask him to hold the tip of your thumb tightly so there is no chance the rope will slip off the top. Then pull both ends, steadily but not jerking them, and the loops will seem to penetrate the thumb and come free.

Another very simple puzzle, but one that those who don't know the secret will have trouble in solving, is the *Scissors and String.* A doubled length of cotton string is fastened through one of the thumb holes of a pair of scissors with a Ring Hitch and the puzzle is to remove the scissors from the string without releasing the ends.

The illustration, Plate Number 7, should make the solution clear. Move the hitch around to the side of the handle as shown and bring the two ends of string through the other handle. Have someone hold the ends. Take the bight of the hitch and bring that down through the handle clear of the held strings. Give your wrist a quarter-turn to pass the bight around the blades and over the scissors as shown by the dotted lines. The scissors now should come off the held string.

A somewhat similar puzzle is the *Ring Off the String,* done with any metal ring or key and a string made into a loop by tying its ends. The string is put through the ring and its two loops held over a person's thumbs as shown in Plate Number 7. The puzzle is to remove the ring without lifting either of the loops from the person's thumbs.

The second drawing shows how it is done. Face the person and have him hold the string slackly. Make a bight with the strand of string *nearest you* and place it over his thumb as shown. Hold it against his thumb with your right hand. Now make a second bight with the strand of string *nearest him* and place that over his same thumb. Have him stretch his arms apart slowly to draw the string taut and the ring will fall from it.

The Patomana Indians of British Guiana have an amusing string puzzle they show as they tell a tall story about a giant fly called a *Toolik.* With a string made from the fiber of the inside bark of a native tree, they work a series of loopings around the thumbs and fingers and draw the hands apart to show the figure of the imaginary fly. They clap the hands together suddenly to trap the big fly, but like any ordinary little housefly, this great giant of all flies is too fast to catch and gets away.

If you want to try to catch a Toolik, start with a piece of string about two yards long. Tie the ends together with a small knot to form an endless loop.

Hold your left hand out in front of you, palm down, fingers pointing to the front, thumb to the right. Slip one end loop of the string over the thumb and bring it across the back of the hand toward the left and out around under the wrist to the right. Hold the right hand with fingers pointed straight up, thumb toward you, palm toward the left. Make sure the two strands of string are not twisted and then hang the other end loop over the right thumb. The two loops remain on the thumbs throughout all the rest of the moves.

With the string in the position given, bring the right hand over to the left and slide your right little finger under the string that crosses the back of your left hand. Catch the two loops over the little finger so the strings come down to the crotch of it and then draw the right hand away. Turn the left hand so that the palms of both hands now face each other, fingers pointed straight up, thumbs toward the rear.

Bring the tip of the left little finger across to the base of the right thumb. Hook the little finger under both strings of the loop that hangs over the right thumb and draw the left hand away pulling the strings back against the finger. Again, hold the hands so the palms face each other.

Now reach with the right hand to the loop that crosses the back of the left wrist. Pull it up over the wrist to the right, free of the left hand, and separate the hands slowly to draw it into a knot midway between them. This is the string picture of the Toolik fly. Drop the loops off your two little fingers and let its "wings" hang down as in the illustration, Plate Number 7.

Tell about the legendary giant fly of British Guiana and how the Indians never could prove he really existed because every time they tried to catch him, he flew away. Clap your hands together smartly and draw them apart and the string Toolik fly will vanish as if he had taken wing.

5

Cowboy Ropes and Lariats

THERE were cowboys because there was rope. Without it, the cattle herdsmen and drovers of the West couldn't have taken to horseback to do the work that would have been impossible for them to do afoot over such vast stretches of land. The lariat was the tool that created the great American cattle ranches and also the men who became glorified in story and legend as "cow boys."

Actually, the first men who called themselves "cow boys" were a band of dairy farmers who raised cows in New York's Westchester County during the Revolutionary War. They were a group of Tories, loyal to the British, who carried out raids against patriots caught between the lines of battle. Years later, soon after Texas became a republic, another band of men operated along the Mexican border, raiding cow farms and capturing cattle, and they too became known as "cow boys."

The name was one which eastern newspaper reporters began to use when they sent back exciting stories about the new ranch life on the western frontier. "Cowboy" gradually came into general use, although some of the early ranch men hotly resented being called "boys." They also were annoyed by adventure novels that pictured them as spending most of their time using their guns and their fists. Rope was something they used far more often.

A cowboy used rope to catch his horse and throw his cattle, to corral animals or pull them out of bog holes when they were stuck, to stake out his horses, pull his wagons across rivers and over rough places, to haul wood to camp and to tie up his bed and fasten his packs. It served as a life-line in snowstorms when he couldn't see his way, helped him fight prairie fires, became a cow whip or snake-killer. The cowboy would have been helpless to do his daily work without it.

Most of the rope used on western ranches was first hemp and later three-strand manila, hard laid for extra strength and smoothness. Some cowboys also made their own rope of rawhide or of horsehair. When they spoke of "doll babies," they were talking about the wooden pegs that were used for making hair ropes.

Hair ropes seldom were used as lariats since they became too kinky and were too light to throw. But braided horsehair cord often served as the bridle for a cowboy's horse or as a tie rope for it. The working horses usually were so well-trained they needed only a very light line to guide them.

Like the sailor who spent his spare time tying fancy knots, the cowboy was likely to amuse himself by making horsehair chains in the form of miniature lariats with hair from his favorite horse's tail. Hours of painstaking work went into them. Some were worn around the neck, reaching down to the vest pocket as a watch chain, to be fastened with a small loop and a Crown Knot to the cowboy's thick gold watch.

Cowboys sometimes carried hair ropes as charms against snakes because there was a widespread belief that no snake would ever crawl across them. Bedding down for the night, when he had to sleep on the ground out in the open, the cowhand would put a circle of horsehair rope around him. However, many a man learned to his sorrow that the snakes had no respect for the legend, since they crawled over horsehair as easily as any other rope.

When he went courting, the cowman might hope to catch his lady love with a miniature horsehair lariat. In some places, a ranch girl who accepted the tiny chain woven from the hair of a man's prized pony was considered pledged to him just as much as the girl of today who accepts a ring or a fraternity pin. When he married, he was said to have "dropped his rope on her."

Rope was so much a part of the cowboy's everyday life that it often flavored the way he spoke. If he said he "shook a rope" at another man, he meant he had given him fair warning. When he beat a fellow cowhand at something, he "took the slack out of his rope," and he would say he meant to "shorten his stake rope" if he intended to do something to put a man at a disadvantage.

While the cowboy's most important use of rope was as a lariat, it is hard to imagine how the old time ranches could have operated without rope as a substitute for fences in the days before barbed wire. The free range area was vast, almost unpopulated and nearly fenceless. Rope, because it could be used to imprison a horse or cow temporarily, took the place of fences.

It was the fear of rope, rather than the rope itself, that kept horses in a temporary corral at a cow camp. Several cowmen might hold the rope stretched between them in a wide-open V shape, or it might be hitched to a line of posts, forked sticks, wagon wheels, or the saddle horns of other horses. All that was needed was one thickness of rope. Free horses, driven up at a gallop to be caught for saddling, would stop at the sight of it.

The horses had learned that rope could catch and throw them and they respected it, especially if the cowhands moved it slightly as a warning. A very loose rope corral would pen the horses long enough for the men to choose those that were wanted and to saddle them for the day's work. Merely dropping the rope would set the others free to go back to pasture.

Pulling mired cattle out of bog holes was a constant rope job for cowboys. Steers looking for water would get stuck in the mud holes or quicksand and had to be pulled to dry land. Cowboys usually worked in pairs to do the job. One might use a short-handled shovel to dig the animal's legs clear while the other hitched a rope around the steer's horns and wrapped the rope end around the horn of his saddle.

The rider would cinch his saddle as tightly as possible and very slowly back his horse, inch by inch, until the bogged down steer was pulled free. He or his partner then "tailed up" the animal by lifting it to its feet by its tail. Usually the ungrateful steer would charge at its rescuers, who had to be quick to get out of the way.

When a cowboy had to tie up his horse for the night while he was out on the range, he usually fastened the rope to a short wooden stake called a "picket pin," which was driven into the ground. The stakes were carried by the chuck wagon.

But if there were no stakes handy, he might just tie a big knot in the end of the rope and bury the knot itself in the ground, stamping down the earth over it, to hold the horse. He seldom used his lariat for a picket rope since he had to tie an extra knot to make a noose that would keep from choking the horse and that kinked the rope so it wasn't much good for catching cattle.

A small soft rope about three feet long was used as a "piggin' string" to hold a calf or young steer that had been thrown to the ground for branding. The animal was kept helpless long enough to do the job by "hog tying" its two hind legs and a front one together. Hog tying has become a regular event in today's rodeo contests.

The man doing the tying has a small loop in one end of the rope, which he slips over the downed animal's foreleg. He stands behind it, with one knee on the animal to help hold it down, and puts his foot under and behind the hocks to boost the hind legs forward. At the same time, he draws the rope under and around both hind feet. With the animal's two hind feet on top and the forefoot below, a few turns of the rope and two Half Hitches leave it well-tied. But a quick slip of the rope will release it again.

Rope helped many a trail wagon across a flooded river during the days of the long drives to bring Texas cattle up to the railroad towns of Kansas for marketing. The drovers couldn't wait for the flood waters to recede and there seldom was a bridge to drive the wagons across. If there were trees available, they cut large logs and lashed them together with rope to make a wagon raft. Sometimes the wagon was partly unloaded and logs were rope-tied to its sides to float it over.

But even when a river was low enough for fording, there often was dangerous quicksand that might trap the wagon wheels. Ropes were then tied to its sides and carried across to trees on the opposite shore. The ropes were brought around the trees so they would take the strain of the pull and then were fastened to the saddle horns of the cowboys' horses. Once the horses began their pull, they couldn't stop for an instant until the wagon was safely across because if the wheels weren't kept rolling they would sink.

On land, when a trail wagon had to go down a steep hill, cowboys often would ride behind with ropes fastened to the top of the load so their ponies could pull back with all their might to keep the wagon from overturning and crashing into some gorge below. They sometimes had to help pull the same wagon back up the next hill, ropes straining taut to their saddle horns.

Cabins and ranch buildings frequently were constructed of rope-hauled logs, dragged over the ground from the woods to the building site, sometimes by a team of horses but often only by a horse-mounted ranch hand and his rope. And the well for water might be dug with the help of the same rope, tied to the top of a small and springy tree that could be bent toward the ground and sprung up and down so the crude drill tool would pound its hole into the earth.

One sure sign of a tenderfoot on the range was a poorly tied Diamond Hitch on a pack horse or mule. It was said that a Westerner meeting a stranger would always take a quick glance at the lashings on his pack saddle before he judged the man. There were many versions of the Diamond Hitch, but most of them had a remarkable ability to hold the load and take up slack. It was a tie that played a major part in Western transportation and nothing so annoyed an old-timer as the sight of a sloppily thrown Diamond Hitch. It was looked on with as much resentment as a badly rigged saddle.

Rope snares were used for catching animals from horseback in various parts of the world for years before the American cowboy came on the scene, but he was the one who developed the Mexican use of the lariat into a highly skilled trade. The word "lariat" comes from the Spanish "la reata" (lah-ray-AH-tah), literally meaning "the tie back."

Southwestern cowboys often called it a "lariat," or sometimes a "reata," but in most other sections of the West it simply was caled a "rope," or perhaps a "ketch rope" if the cowboy wanted to distinguish it from other ropes. Mexicans occasionally used the word "lasso" to mean a long snare line, but the cowboys hardly ever did unless they happened to come from California. Then they might speak of a "lass rope," but were more likely to call it a "riata."

The working catch rope was anywhere from thirty-five to fifty feet or more long and might be up to a half-inch in diameter. During the early days of the West, it generally was made of four strands of buffalo or elk hide, cut in long circular strips one-half inch wide and braided together into rope. The process was a tedious one that required hours of rolling, pounding, boiling and greasing.

Leather lariats were heavy and unwieldy and tended to develop weak spots that gave way, so that the cowboys gladly took to other materials as soon as they were available. Hemp ropes were popular, although they often had to be specially treated to handle equally well in wet or dry weather. Some cowboys preferred catch ropes of maguey, hand-made in Mexico with a smooth and hard finish that would hold a loop. But those weren't considered too good for heavy work. When the commercial ropemakers turned to using manila, so did most of the cowboys.

The method of using the lariat was one of the things that decided its length. Some ropers fastened the rope to the saddle horn by tying it there. The tie-fast men were mostly Texans who worked in a brush country where a throw had to be made almost the instant a steer broke into a clearing. The Texan used a fairly short rope and got close to the animal before spilling his loop. He seldom had much room for a throw or any time to waste in spinning the rope while making it.

In the Northwest and other places where the ranch land was more wide open, with fewer trees and less brush to get in the cowboy's way, the end of rope usually was kept free rather than being tied fast to the saddle. The roper would hold the end in his hand, make his catch with a free-swinging loop from quite a distance away, and then swiftly wind the rope several times around the saddle horn in a counter-clockwise direction to draw it tight and hold it. He could pull it up shorter or release it entirely in an emergency.

This was called "dallying" the rope, from the Spanish phrase "dar la vuelta," which meant to give it a twist or turn. Sometimes the cowboy pronounced it "dolly welter," or he might say he "vuelted" his rope. The dally men used a rope that was nearly twice as long as that of the tie-fast ropers because they needed the extra length to make their dallies. It usually took at least three Half Hitches around the horn to keep the rope from slipping. If a man wound the rope the wrong way, with clockwise turns, he was said to be "coffee grinding."

On a well-run ranch, horses were gentled to the saddle rather than roughly roped and they were seldom thrown the way cattle were. With his neck through the lariat loop, the horse was allowed to prance about the corral, the rope gradually being gathered in to a controlling length. There wasn't much "busting" of good horses because the horse, like the rope, was a tool of work and cowboys didn't want bucking broncs to ride on the job. The "bronc busters" belonged mostly to the early years before ranching was well-established.

The loop of the lariat was formed by passing one end of the rope through the "honda," or eyelet, at the rope's other end.

Sometimes also called a "hondo," this might be merely a knot, an Eye Splice, or a seizing of the rope by whipping it together. It often was lined with smooth leather, a metal ring, or a small brass fixture shaped like an upside-down letter "U" with a bar across the opening. Some men avoided metal hondas because they accidentally might blind the animals they struck.

When not in use, the coiled lariat generally was hung by ties or a strap from below the base of the saddle horn on whichever side its owner found easiest for quick handling. The height, angle and type of the cowboy's saddle were decided by the way he used his lariat. What he called the "postage stamp" saddle of the Easterner couldn't be used for roping. The cowboy needed a saddle with enough of a horn for the rope, a back that would hold him, and sturdy construction to withstand the terrific strain.

All cowboys wore gloves in cold weather and nearly always for roping. Many of them kept gloves on their hands no matter what the weather or the job they were doing. During roping, gloves were necessary to prevent burns and blisters. Many expert ropers were vain about keeping their hands as white and soft as a young girl's.

The gloves generally were of high quality buckskin, gray or yellow, and treated so they wouldn't stiffen when wet because a stiff glove might misdirect the throw of the lariat. They usually had flaring cuffs, often embroidered with silken thread in elaborate designs. Sometimes cowboys wore stiff leather cuffs to protect their wrists and also garters on their sleeves to pull them tight and keep them from getting in the way.

It took years of practice for a man to become an expert roper. Roping was highly dangerous work and needed not only great skill, but also split-second timing and the ability to out-guess the running animal that was to be snared, a kind of rope sense that came only after long experience. But as good as a man might become, as much depended on the training of his rope horse.

A horse specially trained to the work knew what to do with only the slightest signal. As soon as the catch was made, the horse would sit back, feet braced to take the shock, ready at the touch of the reins to whirl and face the catch.

The good rope horse would never let a cow run to his side or let the rope slacken to trip him up. As soon as the cowboy took his rope in hand, the horse knew what was expected. He would run to the left side of the cow, wait for the throw, know whether it had caught or missed, and then pull against the rope to drag the animal's dead weight along the ground.

During the spring roundups, cowboys would worm their way through the herd, separating the animals to be branded or sold from the others. This was called "cutting out" and meant that the cowhand would ride between the wanted animal and the rest of the cattle, his pony twisting and dodging in and out to clear the calf or steer from the others so the lariat could be used.

Chasing after the cut-out animal, the cowboy would take his coiled lariat from the saddle and hold it high with his left hand. Gripping the honda with his right hand, he would pay out enough of the rope to make a proper noose, shaking it through the honda with short jerks of his wrist. When he had formed a circle of rope about six feet around, he would grasp the rope some twenty inches or so behind the honda with his palm-down right hand, holding both sides of the noose and the part of the rope that hadn't already passed through the honda.

He would swing the noose over his head three or four times until it took an oval shape and keep it spinning out flat above him until the instant before the throw was made. Then he would whirl it with tremendous speed, twisting his right shoulder back and drawing his right hand to the rear so it could shoot forward and release the noose. It might be thrown over the animal's head or spun out to strike the ground and bounce up to catch its legs. As the lariat began to jerk taut, it was snubbed around the saddle horn.

The pony would shift one way or the other, bracing against the threshing pull of the thrown animal to hold the beast until the other men could hog-tie it or pin it down. As soon as it was under control, the rope would be released so the cowboy could be off after another wanted animal. Sometimes the cowboy himself would "go down the rope" to the steer he had spilled and hog-tie it, doing the whole job in a matter of seconds. He worked at lightning speed against the bawling, thundering noise and in clouds of choking dust.

Dust was even more of a problem to the cowboy who rode as "drag man" or "tail rider" on the long drives up the trails to Kansas. With a knotted neckerchief covering his nose and mouth, he had to fight for his breath against the stinging dust as he rode back and forth at the very rear of the herd, keeping the lazy and footsore animals from dropping back or lying down and refusing to go on.

The drag man's lariat often had a long buckskin "popper" spliced into it. With an underhand throw and a snap of his wrist, he could shoot out some twenty feet of rope and crack the popper at its end to make it sound like a pistol shot that would keep a lagging steer on the move.

Cowboys had many ways, of course, of throwing a lariat. Some made fast throws and others seemed to drop slow and almost lazy-looking loops. It was a job, not an exhibition of fancy roping, and all that counted was the catch. But in their spare time, cowboys constantly were trying trick stunts with lariats, just for the fun of it. And a lonely man, riding along on his horse, was likely to throw his rope at nearly anything that moved.

Some even tried to snare grizzly bears or buffalo and legend has it that more than one impulsive cowboy tossed his loop over the smokestack of a moving locomotive. In such cases, he usually had sense enough to let go of his end of the rope in a hurry. But he might spend hours throwing his rope over a bush or a post for his own amusement.

Trick catch roping and lariat spinning gradually became a sport and a form of entertainment at the roundups. Sometimes contests of roping skill, as well as skill in riding horses and handling cattle, were held among the cowboys who gathered from the various ranches to get the steers ready for marketing.

Bets often were made and the ranchers occasionally chipped in to offer prizes. Out of such contests came the rodeos and Wild West shows.

Mexicans who spoke of the rounding up of cattle used the Spanish word "rodear," which meant to encircle, and the Californians who picked up the use of the word pronounced it "rodeo." The first public roping and riding contests for cash prizes began in the late 1800's in Texas, Arizona and Wyoming. But the great rodeo spectacles which now attract millions of people throughout the country each year, offering a living to hundreds of free-lance contestants who travel the circuit trying for prizes, really began their growth in the 1920's.

It was the Wild West shows, which became an entertainment rage before the turn of the century, that gave the trick ropers and spinners their start as paid performers. Colonel George W. Miller, who founded the famous old 101 Ranch of Oklahoma in 1878, put on a cowboy show in Winfield, Kansas, in 1882.

The next year, Colonel William F. Cody, better known as Buffalo Bill, organized his Wild West Rocky Mountain and Prairie Exhibition in North Platte, Nebraska. It had its first big tryout in Brooklyn, New York, and there were soon dozens of imitators, touring like circuses to play in canvas-walled arenas throughout the United States and in foreign lands.

One of the stars of the Buffalo Bill show was the great Mexican roper, Vincenti Orespo, who featured sensational rope catches in his act and also demonstrated fancy spinning tricks. He sometimes is credited with originating modern rope spinning, which became a standard part of show business in circuses and cowboy spectacles and in vaudeville. While catch roping is a direct outgrowth of the cowboy's daily work, fancy rope spinning has no practical use on the range and is strictly a performance, like juggling.

The most famous of all ropers was, of course, the celebrated cowboy philosopher, Will Rogers. His spinning ropes and wit brought him international fame and made him such a beloved idol of all America that even today, a quarter of a century after his death, thousands of people pay tribute to his memory by visiting the Will Rogers Memorial at Claremore, Oklahoma, every day of the year.

He was a rancher, roper, Wild West and circus performer, vaudeville actor, Broadway and Hollywood star, comedian, radio commentator, newspaper columnist, lecturer and author. People would drop whatever they were doing to hear his latest comments on national and international affairs and his remarks, often penetratingly shrewd as well as witty, were held in respect by most of the world's leaders who called him friend. He was a pal of presidents and cowhands alike and twice was suggested as a possible candidate for the presidency himself.

Will Rogers was born in 1879 in his father's ranch house halfway between Claremore and Oologah in what was then Indian Territory. He said later that he claimed Claremore as his birthplace because "nobody but an Indian can pronounce Oologah." Because he was simple in his speech and his manner and never cared much about the clothes he wore, many people thought he was a poor and uneducated cowboy. Actually, his father was one of the wealthiest men in the Territory.

Both his parents were part Cherokee Indian. Will's father, in addition to being a well-to-do rancher, became a banker and statesman prominent in the affairs of the Cherokee nation and was a member of the Constitutional Convention that framed the laws for Oklahoma statehood. If anything, Will was spoiled by too much of having his own way as a young boy. He was a disappointment to his parents in school, wouldn't settle down to his responsibilities, and seemed to have no great interest in anything but spinning a rope.

He could do that nearly as well as any man around by the time he was twelve. Will spent almost all his time at it, riding his pony and trying to rope just about everything in sight. If anybody could show him a rope trick he didn't know, he would hang around until he learned it.

When he was first sent away to school at the age of thirteen, he took his lariat with him, much to the dislike of his teachers. He not only neglected his lessons for it, but also hid it in his desk in class so he could drop a loop on the floor to catch the legs of other students who walked past.

There was a pasture near the school and Will put on impromptu shows of his rope tricks there. He also took part in school plays and when he went back home, he liked to stand out in front of the store at Oologah and show off his skill to the townsfolk. Will had one of the first bicycles in the Indian Territory and he even tried roping calves from that.

His parents sent him to a military academy in the hope that his schooling would improve and also with the idea that he would leave his lariat at home. But he turned up with it tied around his trunk. To get it past the professors so he could go out to practice spinning it, he sometimes concealed it wrapped around himself under his clothes. He paid some of the younger boys twenty-five cents an hour to let him rope them. They got a lot of bruises and rope burns, but seemed to enjoy the fun as much as he did.

Will spent two years at the academy, as he later put it, "one in the guardhouse and the other in fourth grade." He said that he might have gone on to West Point if he hadn't been too proud to speak to a Congressman. As it was, he quit school and tried his hand at ranching and trail driving. He won first prize in a Fourth of July roping contest put on at Claremore in 1899, and not long after that he took part in a fair at St. Louis.

The fair was managed by Colonel Zach Mulhall, a livestock agent for the Rock Island Railroad, who promoted Wild West exhibitions and ran special excursion trains to bring people to them from miles around. Mulhall gave Will his first real introduction to show business and, as he jokingly explained, "I was ruined for life as far as actual work was concerned." He soon was showing his roping at every fair and contest he could find.

He heard of a big Confederate veterans' reunion that was to be held at Memphis, Tennessee, and talked the officials into letting him stage a riding and roping show. With forty riders, horses and cattle rounded up at home, he presented a pageant complete with Indian war dances and a grand parade. It lasted for four days and was a big success with the crowd, but he came home broke, having spent too much to make any profit.

Too restless to settle down and take over his share of the home ranch, he headed for New York, traveled around awhile and then went to South America where he took a job as a gaucho on an Argentine cattle ranch. It was adventure he wanted, not money, since the work paid only four dollars a month. He heard of a chance to go to South Africa with a cattle shipment and jumped at that.

When he arrived with the cattle, he discovered there was a Wild West show playing near the South African town of Lady-smith. Homesick by then, Will made friends with the owner of the show, Texas Jack. He was offered a job as a roper, but his duties also included riding a bucking bronc and taking the part of an Indian in a play that depicted Western life.

Playing one-day stands, sometimes to audiences of African natives, he amused himself by trying his hand at roping zebras, among other things. But he gave most of his time to learning new rope tricks that won him featured billing as "The Cherokee Kid." He had trouble finding the kind of rope he needed and wrote home to his father to send him some of the best hard-twist rope he could find.

"I can't get a thing here that we use," he wrote. "Some nights I rope with old tie ropes or any old thing. Please send this at once, the quickest, fastest and shortest way, no matter what the cost."

But, good rope or not, he justified his billing and became star of the show. He had cards and letterheads printed, advertising himself as a fancy rope artist: "The Cherokee Kid—the man who can lasso the tail off a blowfly!" Show business had become his way of life and he explained in a later letter home that "this might not be the best business, but there is good money and it's honest." He told his father he intended to learn all he could about it, so he could earn his way in the world "without making it by day labor."

He left Texas Jack to join the Wirth Brothers Circus and to tour Australia and New Zealand as "The Mexican Rope Artist," wearing a red velvet suit that was gaudily trimmed with gold braid. After some fifty thousand miles of travel, he finally returned to San Francisco. His father wanted him to stay home, but Will went to St. Louis to try out his act in a vaudeville theater.

During an appearance in Chicago, a dog broke loose from one of the animal acts on the bill with him. Will tossed his rope and caught the dog, much to the amusement of the applauding audience. He began working on a routine in which a running horse would be caught on the stage, something that had never been done before. Meanwhile, his old friend, Colonel Mulhall, invited him to join a Western exhibition that was to be put on at New York's Madison Square Garden in connection with the National Horse Show.

Will thought it was his big break, that his success would be made, but even though he got his name in the newspapers by roping a wild steer that charged into the audience during the show, he found it as hard as ever to land bookings for his act. Day after day, he made the weary rounds of the theatrical agencies and then journeyed over to nearby New Jersey to practice his riding and roping.

He appeared in small vaudeville theaters and slowly worked his way into the big time. Will's act started with a display of fancy roping, performed silently with a number of soft cotton ropes of different lengths, each perfectly balanced for the trick in which it was used. They were kept ready for him in neat coils just behind the footlights. His horse came on then and he did a series of catches with a heavier, more tightly woven Kentucky hemp rope.

The act ended with the spinning of a big loop called a "Crinoline," in which a rope one hundred feet long was used. Will handed one end of the rope to an usher and asked him to back down the aisle to the rear of the theater to show how long it was. He then mounted his horse and began spinning, gradually letting out the rope until it was whirling in a huge circle over the heads of the audience.

When he first decided to talk, to explain some of his tricks, he was hurt because people laughed at his drawling remarks. He wanted to be applauded as a roper, not a comedian. But other actors appearing with him advised him to make the most of the laughter and he began to work hard over funny things to say. His jokes were written out and memorized at first, not impromptu, and some were written for him.

But as he began to gain in showmanship, he found his own natural style of wit. He took the basic truth of a situation and exaggerated it until people laughed. It was a type of humor that required more than just jokes. He was a keen analyst of current affairs and seemed to be able to put into words just what most people wished they were clever enough to say about things happening in the world.

It was while he was appearing in the Ziegfeld Follies that he began to introduce his remarks with the phrase that became famous, "I see by the papers. . . ." He read the papers constantly and always had up-to-the-minute comments to make, unlike other comedians who repeated their material from one show to the next. People began to come back to see his act time and again and his popularity grew.

Will married Betty Blake in 1908, during his struggling days in vaudeville. After he became a Broadway star, he and his wife moved to Long Island, near the home of his close friend, actor Fred Stone. He kept up his roping practice there and often had fun teaching the neighborhood children, who soon began to appropriate every clothesline in sight to imitate the tricks he showed them. During a swimming accident, his right arm was temporarily paralyzed and he had to learn to do all his roping with his left hand so as to keep his act going.

Even after he became more celebrated as a wit than a roper, when nearly every newspaper in the land was eager to quote what he had to say, Will spent almost all his spare time with his spinning ropes. He took them along on his lecture tours and usually ended his talks with a display of fancy roping. The ropes were scrubbed after each performance and bleached so they would show up well. When he had a day off, he spent it roping.

During the height of his success as a Hollywood movie star, he kept his ropes handy in a closet so he and a few friends could get them out on Sunday afternoons to toss loops at the living room furniture. While he was working on a picture, he often insisted on quitting his day's acting so he could get home in time to rope a few calves on his ranch.

Between pictures and all the other activities that kept him busy, he frequently spent his time riding and roping with cowhands and other old pals while celebrities waited for a chance to speak to him. He was never awed by the other famous people who claimed him as a friend and had little use for pomp and ceremony.

When the move to nominate him as a candidate for President became serious, he tried to turn it down as a joke, saying that the country hadn't become so sad it needed a professional comedian in the White House. During the Democratic convention in 1932, when his name was offered, Will pretended to sleep through the proceedings.

He raised hundreds of thousands of dollars for humanitarian causes, earned himself a huge personal fortune and won fame throughout the world with only his ropes and his wit. Among his enthusiasms was flying and he did as much as any private citizen could to advance the popularity of air travel. It was during a flight in Alaska in 1935 with aviator Wiley Post that he lost his life in a plane crash.

Three years later, the state of Oklahoma erected the $200,000 memorial at Claremore on land he had bought years earlier to build a home. Its spacious galleries overlook Rogers County and hold the saddles and trappings, some of the original manuscripts, and other belongings that were his, as well as paintings and tributes to the man who caught the affection of millions with his spinning ropes and cowboy wisdom.

CATCH ROPING (See Plate Number 8)

CATCH ROPING has very little in common with rope spinning. The idea in catch roping is to throw a lariat in such a way that the noose encircles an animal or some other object and tightens around it. In rope spinning, the loop is kept open and not thrown to catch anything, but is merely whirled rapidly to display various fancy formations and tricks that can be done as it spins.

Most of us never expect to rope a horse or a steer, but there is a lot of fun to be had from the sport of lariat throwing. It is easier to learn than rope spinning, can be enjoyed indoors in a club room or gymnasium as well as outdoors in a field or back yard, and it also has some practical uses aside from those the cowboy puts it to.

The ability to throw a rope noose around something beyond reach comes in handy in climbing, on camping trips, in boating, and for dozens of jobs of lifting or pulling with rope, as well as for an emergency when somebody in the water or in other trouble needs a lifeline.

It takes long practice, of course, before anybody can drop a loop accurately every time over a moving target. But the simplest form of catch roping can be learned in a few hours so that it can be done passably well, just for the fun of it. Some people who have never handled a rope before are able to toss a loop over a post or a chair on the third or fourth try. But like any sport, the fun increases as the knack is learned through regular practice.

The Catch Rope and the Target

Although a thick and fairly stiff clothesline will do if there is nothing else to be had, the best rope for learning is ordinary ⅜″ manila, available in most hardware stores. Professional catch ropes, such as those sold by suppliers of Western and dude ranch equipment, usually are too stiff for the beginner. Toy lariats sometimes offered in dime stores generally are too light for catch roping.

The rope should be about thirty-five feet long. A honda must be made in one end. This can be done by making an Eye Splice or by fastening it with friction tape or thin wire, but the simplest way is to tie a Honda Knot, as explained in Chapter Three.

It should be tied about ten inches from the end, the knot jammed as tightly as possible, and then the other end of the rope put through the wide-open eye. Tape should be wound around the free end of rope to keep it from unraveling.

Metal hondas are dangerous to use in learning to rope because they may cause injuries. A pair of rather tight-fitting old gloves may be worn to avoid rope burns and splinters, although they may not be necessary in the first stages of practice with a still target. But wearing old clothes is a good idea because the rope will pick up dirt from the ground or the floor.

There must be enough room for the throw, at least twenty feet in the beginning and more as you become better at it. A good practice target is an old kitchen chair, one that can take a little rough handling, preferably the kind with a straight back and no arms. Outdoors a post planted in the ground so it stands three or four feet high is an excellent target.

Small animals, such as cats and dogs, should not be roped by a beginner, nor should people serve as casual targets. Properly used there is hardly any danger that anyone will be hurt with a catch rope, but a squeezing noose may injure a small animal and people unexpectedly caught on the run may be tripped and take bad spills. Even the expert roper uses common sense in tossing his loop at anything. He knows it has the power to throw a heavy steer right off its feet.

Coiling the Catch Rope

Coiling the rope so it will run out freely and easily when thrown is so important that it is worth careful practice before any catches are attempted. Whether the rope is in use or is to be put aside ready for use, proper coiling should become a habit.

Start by laying out the rope on the ground so it is free of kinks. The eye of the honda should be at the left end as you stand behind the rope. Pick up the honda and bring the free end through it to form a six-foot noose. Now hold it with the right hand as shown in Plate Number 8. Notice that the honda is on the outside and that the free end runs straight through it and isn't doubled back over it. The rope should be held so the honda is a foot or two below the hand.

With the left hand, bring up the rest of the rope, making coils about fifteen inches in diameter until the end of it is reached. The coils may be a little awkward to make at first, especially with new rope which tends to kink. Some of this can be avoided by giving the rope a little twist by rolling the left thumb in toward yourself as each coil is placed in the right hand. This will help make the coils lie flat.

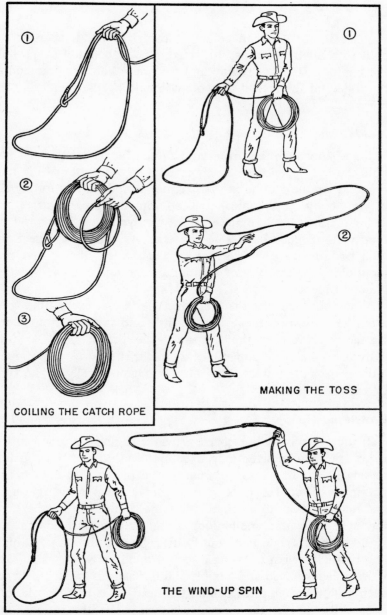

① ② ③

COILING THE CATCH ROPE

① ②

MAKING THE TOSS

THE WIND-UP SPIN

PLATE № 8   CATCH ROPING

After it has all been coiled in the right hand, transfer the coils to the left hand, as illustrated. The right hand keeps only the big loop. The left thumb and forefinger hold the free end of the rope and the rest of the coils are held by the remaining left fingers.

Making the Toss

Stand about ten feet from your target, facing it squarely, and hold the loop open with the right hand so the center of the loop is spread on the ground at your right side and slightly to the rear of your body. (See Plate 8.) Keep your eye on the target and swing the arm forward and upward past your side, throwing the loop with an underhand side-arm toss. As you release it, swing your body forward with a long step of the left foot to give momentum to the throw. Let additional rope uncoil from your left hand as necessary.

When you can toss the loop over the target every time from a ten-foot distance, move back a little and practice from there, gradually increasing the length of the throw. The Toss, or "Ground Toss" as it sometimes is called, is used by most ropers afoot, especially for handling horses that might shy at the sight of a spinning lariat.

The Wind-Up Spin

If the roper is on horseback or wants to make a much longer throw, he may spin the loop over his head several times before tossing it, winding up somewhat as the ball player does before making his pitch. He starts by arranging the loop in his right hand and holding it out to his right side as he would for the other toss, but he begins with a smaller loop, about four feet instead of six.

He keeps his right hand out to his right side, lifts it head-high, and twists his wrist to swing a loop around above his head. The wrist is kept relaxed and flexible and the hand is twisted palm up each time the rope spins behind the head so as to keep the loop open and ready for the throw, as shown in the illustration, Plate Number 8.

The swing is made in a direction from right to left. As the loop swings around, the roper can increase the size of it by releasing his fingers a little so that the momentum pulls more of the rope through.

Instead of trying to toss the loop over the target, he pitches the rope right at it. The throw is overhand, just as though a ball were being thrown.

ROPE SPINNING (See Plate Number 9)

ROPE SPINNING was once done mostly by professional entertainers, but rodeos and dude ranches helped develop it as the sport it is today, enjoyed by many roping clubs, school and camp groups and other amateurs. The basic spins have become standard in pattern, just as the figures in ice skating are. Some are fairly easy to learn with a little patience and practice. But skill in rope spinning, as in any sport, is something that comes gradually.

The spinning rope is shorter than the catch rope, usually from about fifteen to twenty feet in length. Since it serves an entirely different purpose, a different kind of rope is needed, one in which the loop will hold open rather than draw tight. It is handled in such a way that the loop remains circular while it is swung. The revolving spin and the friction of the honda against the rope keep the loop from collapsing.

Many beginners become discouraged because they use the wrong kind of rope. Some kinds of clothesline and other rope just won't spin well in anybody's hands. Even an expert would have trouble with them.

What is usually recommended for spinning is Number 12 solid-braided cotton sashcord, which is three-eighths of an inch thick and stiff enough to hold the loop without loosening or becoming softened with use. It is inexpensive and sold in most hardware stores.

Professional ropers often use what is called "Spot Cord," or else an even harder-braided cord made especially for spinning which is known as "Spot Lariat Cord," both of which are named for the colored spots they have to identify them.

Making a Spinning Lariat

Spinning lariats may be bought ready-made, but it is easy to make your own with a length of the right kind of rope and some medium-weight copper wire. The wire is needed for the honda and for binding the end of the rope so it won't unravel.

The parts of the spinning rope and the threading of it are shown in Plate Number 9. To make the honda, double back one end of the rope so it forms an eye with an opening about two inches long and secure the end to the rope with five or six turns of the wire, wrapping the wire around tightly. Now wrap two or three turns of wire around the other end of the rope, put that end through the honda, and the rope is ready.

Spinning a Flat Loop

The Flat Loop is considered the simplest of all rope spins, but a number of more elaborate tricks are based on it and the beginner should learn to do it with ease before he goes on to anything else.

Arrange the rope as shown in the first of the drawings for the Flat Loop in Plate Number 9. The rope end is held between the right thumb and forefinger while the rest of the right-hand fingers hold the loop and the left hand spreads it open. Make sure the honda is well down the side of the loop so as to give it a spoke that is about as long as one-half the diameter of the loop. The hands should be well below the waist and the spinner should lean forward slightly at the hips.

Spinning requires a slow and gentle motion, not a rapid whirling around of the hand. Any quick jerk or excited action will make the loop collapse. Once the spin has started, it is kept going with an easy and rhythmic turning of the wrist.

The starting moves should be practiced step by step until

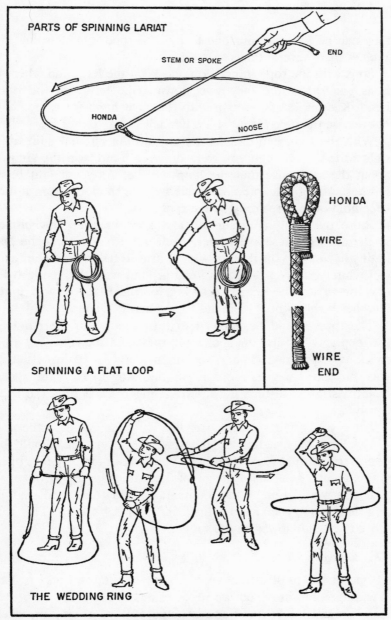

PARTS OF SPINNING LARIAT

END

STEM OR SPOKE

HONDA

NOOSE

HONDA

WIRE

WIRE END

SPINNING A FLAT LOOP

THE WEDDING RING

PLATE Nº 9   ROPE SPINNING

they can be blended into one to put the rope into its spin. Try each of them several times to get the hang of it.

Start with the rope in position and keep the left hand where it is as you throw the loop over toward the left with the right hand. Keep hold of the loop with the right hand for a moment, but release the rope from the left hand.

With the right hand, make a slow and flat circular spin from right to left, as though you were drawing a circle in the air just about the same size that the loop will be. As your right hand finishes cutting this complete circle, release the loop from it and keep hold of the rope only by the spoke.

Raise the right hand slightly and keep making slow circles in the air with it several times, each one smaller than the last until you can stop the motion of your arm. Finally, hold your arm still while you keep the rope going around with the gentle twist of your wrist. The second drawing for the Flat Loop in Plate Number 9 shows how it should look when it is spun.

The rope should be allowed to turn around in the hand as the loop spins or else the spoke will twist and the rope will kink so it stops spinning. Hold it very lightly and let it turn itself in your fingers as it goes around. Another way to keep the spoke from twisting is to turn it with your fingers each time the rope revolves.

After you get it spinning steadily, you can increase the size of the loop by speeding up the spin. However, this should be done very gradually. As you move your wrist more rapidly, open your spinning hand and let some of the extra rope slip through.

If you want to make the loop smaller, slow its speed slightly and then lower your hand a little and pull it back up. This will move the honda lower on the spoke.

The Wedding Ring

One of the most attractive of all rope spinning tricks is The Wedding Ring, in which the roper stands inside a flat loop that spins around his body. It can be done on foot or on horseback and is the basis for many acrobatic and juggling stunts with the spinning rope. When a very long rope is used, it becomes the Crinoline, which was featured by Will Rogers and other famous ropers.

A rope about twenty feet long should be used for The Wedding Ring. The illustration, Plate Number 9, shows how it should be arranged, with the end of the spoke in the right hand and the honda down at the ground while the left hand holds the loop open.

The right hand picks up the loop and turns it back over the head, as illustrated, with an easy and graceful motion that is slow and deliberate. The left hand is kept at waist level and must not be raised while this is being done. The right hand lets the loop fall around the body and drop to the waist.

Both hands then give the loop a circular spin around the body from right to left and release the loop, the right hand keeping hold only of the end of the spoke. The right hand is raised around behind the head, then up over the head, and keeps the loop spinning with a gentle wrist motion.

When the hand finally is in position above the head, the arm must be kept from making any wide swinging motion. It should remain still, letting just the thumb and finger guide the rope in its spin while a very slight swaying of the body keeps it going around.

Again, the starting movements should be learned step by step, through trial and error, until they can be blended smoothly. The mistake most beginners make is in taking the moves too rapidly and especially in not allowing enough time for the loop to settle down at waist level. Slow counting to yourself to time the actions may help.

Remember always to hold the rope lightly and to do the whole thing in a relaxed and easy manner. And also accept the fact that your first efforts are almost sure to fail. Your rope probably will wind up in a tangled mess. But the trick really is not difficult to do, once you begin to understand it from trying. When you master it, you will have learned one of the best rope tricks anybody can perform.

6

Rope Crafts and Games

THE crafts of making things with rope are many, from the sailor's fancy knot work and sennits to the cord-weaving of the netmaker and the braiding ability of the Indian and the cowboy.

Some are difficult and may well be left to the expert or to the person willing to spend months learning them. However, there are many attractive and useful things to be made of rope without expert skill.

Rope Handles

Sailors put rope handles on nearly everything from sea chests to wooden buckets. The idea can be borrowed to dress up an old bureau or chest of drawers to give it a distinctive appearance. It is easy to put rope handles on the drawers.

Assuming that you have permission to do the job, all that is necessary is to bore two holes in the front of the drawer. Very often you can make use of the holes already there for the metal handle or knobs the drawer originally had. Simply bore them larger. Then cut pieces of rope to the length desired, put the ends through the holes and knot them inside the drawer with an Overhand Knot in each end.

Manila rope makes sturdy drawer handles and adds a nautical or Western touch to any room or den. Cotton rope may be dyed with ordinary textile dyes to any color to match a room's decorations. Rope handles also serve well on work-bench drawers, under-bed storage boxes, cellar or attic hatch covers and on the doors of vacation cabins.

Rope Ladder Bookshelves

Another of the sailor's crafts, the making of rope ladders, can be turned to good home use in constructing simple wall shelves for books or collected items to be displayed.

Get three or four boards the size of the shelves you want, or have your local lumber yard cut them to size, and bore a hole through each corner of them. Fasten two screw-eyes to the wall above where you want to hang the shelves and cut two lengths of rope slightly more than twice as long as the total height of the shelves.

Thread one end of one of the ropes through the holes at the rear left corner of one of the boards and tie a firm stopper knot at the end of the rope. Measure out the rope to where the next shelf will be, tie another knot and then thread the rope up through that board. Continue with the rest of the shelves. Now do the same thing on the other side.

Bring the ropes up through the screw-eyes that are fastened to the wall and then down through the holes in the front of the shelves, adjusting each and tying a knot beneath each board. The shelves, when they are finished, should look like those illustrated in Plate Number 10. They may be of any height or length, of course, but make sure that the rope, knots and screw-eyes are firm enough to hold whatever weight you intend to put on them.

A Rope Bed

Cowboys and Western pioneers often used rope to make the "springs" of their beds. With an old wooden bed frame, or a new one made to measure if you have home carpentering skill, it is fairly simple to make a rope spring for a camp cot or a bunk in a den. Bore holes along the sideboards four inches apart, as shown in Plate Number 10. Holes should be drilled six inches apart in the end boards.

Use one single length of rope. Knot it inside the frame at one side. Then bring it out and back through the next hole on that same side. Draw it tight and bring it across to a hole on the other side, continuing until you get to the other end of the bed. Now repeat the process in a lengthwise direction, but thread the rope over and under each alternate cross-rope. The final knot also should be tied on the inside of the frame.

Home Safety Tricks with Rope

Many homes have cellar stairs made of open planks as steps. These may be given a safety tread for surer footing merely by winding a length of rope flatly around each of them. Start by

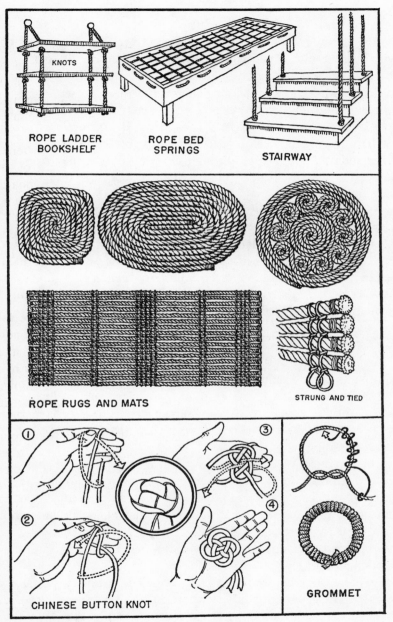

ROPE LADDER BOOKSHELF

KNOTS

ROPE BED SPRINGS

STAIRWAY

ROPE RUGS AND MATS

STRUNG AND TIED

① ② ③ ④

CHINESE BUTTON KNOT

GROMMET

PLATE Nº 10

fastening one end of the rope firmly on the underside of the step with large staples. Then wind it around the step tightly, continue the parallel windings across the center, and staple the other end underneath when the tread has reached the width desired.

The same thing may be done to give safety treads to the home step-ladder or to a flat-topped foot stool. If you are making a kitchen or garage shelf for the storage of bottles, paint cans or other such things, wrapping rough-finish cord or twine around it before the shelf is fixed in place will help keep the things from slipping off.

An open-sided stairway which has no railing may be enclosed with lengths of rope in the manner shown in Plate Number 10. All that is needed is a large screw-eye in each step and another fastened to the sidewall directly above. Lengths of rope are then tied between to reach toward the ceiling from each step. The ends are knotted to the screw-eyes and then finished off with a binding of small copper wire or a neat seizing of strong waxed thread.

Rope Garden Crafts

An inexpensive and unusual garden trellis for climbing flowers and plants can be made by attaching screw-eyes both at top and bottom to a wooden frame or to two wooden bars fastened between upright posts. A pleasing arrangement is to place two screw-eyes side by side about three inches apart on the top bar and a matching set at the bottom.

Run a length of rope from the left screw-eye at the bottom up through the two at the top and back down to the right one at the bottom. Then place additional sets of screw-eyes and ropes a foot or so apart, according to the needs of whatever plants will grow up them. Instead of the straight up-and-down arrangement, the ropes may be criss-crossed if you wish, as in the conventional wooden trellis.

Fences also may be made with rope and wooden posts, in short lengths as yard dividers or wherever small garden enclosures are needed. In addition to being distinctive looking, they have the advantage of never needing paint since weathering adds to their appearance. Sturdy log posts give the fencing a rustic look. They should be firmly embedded.

Rope may be run straight across from post to post and knotted at the sides of each post hole. A little slack should be allowed for weather-tightening. Another arrangement is to run the ropes in a criss-cross fashion, by boring diagonal holes through the posts and lacing the rope back across from one end to the other.

Still simpler is a rope fence made with an oblong wooden frame equipped with screw-eyes top and bottom as in the trellis. These may be spaced so the rope can be threaded up and down in a continuous lacing formed like: VVVVVVV.

Driveway name signs made of rope are different. With a thick lead pencil, print or write your family name in letters about four inches high on the sign board which is to be used. Lightly drive nails in sets of two around the letters. Coat over the penciled lettering with glue and work the rope around through the nails to fasten it to the board.

Remove each set of nails, replacing them with a staple firmly driven home to help hold the rope in position. Coat the entire board with a colorless plastic spray paint and then screw it to an upright pointed stake for planting beside the driveway or at the front walk.

If you wish, the rope may be coated with luminous paint to show up at night, or wrapped around with night-glow adhesive tape before it is stapled to the board. Rope signs also make interesting direction markers at camp. For additional decoration, they may have a border of ornamental knots stapled around them.

Mats and Rugs

An easy way to make a rope rug or mat is to take a length of rope and wind it in a flat coil from the center out, sewing the coils together with a large needle and heavy thread.

Start with the rope on the floor or on a large table. Turn the rope end upon itself as tightly as you can, make a flat turn around that, and sew the two together by passing the needle through the centers of the rope. A block of wood to press the end of the needle against will help push it through. Sew it in several places and then coil the rope another turn and repeat the sewing.

If you find it too difficult to sew through the centers of rope, the edges may be stitched together with a simple cross-stitch, but this makes a less sturdy construction. The sewing must be done evenly so the rug will lie flat when completed. If the work is done on a large board, small nails may be used to hold the initial coils in place. Some rope rug-makers form all the coils first, then stitch across them from one to the next. After the sewing is finished, the rope should be turned on its other side for use.

Instead of a round rug, one of oblong or oval shape can be made by starting with a small oblong or oval in the center rather than a circle. Various center designs also may be made, either with the same rope or with separate lengths of a different color, by forming coils or squares inside the larger winding and sewing them into place. Plate Number 10 shows several types of rope rugs.

A square or oblong rug can be made of separate lengths of rope laid parallel and bound together with twine or string instead of sewing them. The binding strings may be in contrasting color, if desired.

Start by cutting the rope into the separate pieces of whatever length the rug is to be. Lay one piece of rope on the floor and double a string to fasten it around the rope with a Ring Hitch a few inches from the rope's end. Fasten three more strings in the same way beside the first one.

Come along the rope six inches and fasten another set of four more strings. Do this four, six or eight times, depending on the length of the rug. Straighten out the strings so they all run vertical to the horizontal rope.

Now put down a second length of rope parallel to the first. Bring one end of *each* pair of strings under the rope and the other end over the rope. Cross them and draw the strings tight. When that has been done with all the sets of strings down the line, add another length of rope, and so on.

When the rug is complete, bring the ends of all strings around the edge and pass them back down through between the last two lengths of rope. Knot them off there on what will be the reverse side of the rug.

Rugs and mats may be made in any size desired. Small ones make good-looking coasters for drinking glasses. Others will make place mats for the table. Still larger ones can be used as bathroom mats or throw rugs. Rope makes excellent mats for puppies, kittens and other small pets.

The most durable rope for mats and rugs is manila, but cotton is easier to sew and can be dyed various colors. Plastic cord, raffia, leather or other materials may be used. A fairly large throw rug will require several hundred feet of rope while a coaster will take only a few feet. The length needed will depend, of course, on the diameter of the rope chosen.

Decorating with Rope and Cord

Old bottles may be made into interesting looking vases and lamp bases by winding small rope or cord around them as a covering.

Use an artist's paint brush to coat the bottle with thick glue in circles around it as you wind the rope from the bottom up. If the rope is tightly wound, friction will help hold it in place until the glue sets. When you get to the end at the top of the winding, bind that to the coil beneath it with copper wire. Waste baskets, wooden boxes and even large tin cans may be decorated in the same way.

For Christmas, cotton ropes dyed red or silver make an unusual tree decoration. They may be draped on the tree branches in plain garlands or tied in chains of fancy knots. Small gifts can be wound in the centers of balls of cord hung on the tree as ornaments, to be unwound to disclose the surprises they hold.

Knots for Buttons

Knots make good buttons for winter coats, car coats, sports jackets and Western type clothing. Two simple Square Knots tied on top of each other in the center of a short length of cord, with an Overhand Knot tied on top of those and all of them jammed tightly together, will make a practical button.

The two ends of cord may be drawn through the material and knotted on the inside or they may be sewn to the outside to replace the original button. The existing buttonhole can be used or a doubled length of cord sewn on the opposite side will serve as a loop for buttoning.

A more ornamental button can be made with the *Chinese Button Knot.* This is one of the hundreds of button knots used by sailors in their fancy knotting. The Chinese use it on their night clothes because it is more comfortable to lie on than regular hard buttons and it doesn't break when things are laundered.

To tie it, follow the diagrams for the Chinese Button Knot in Plate Number 10. Put the center of a cord about three feet long over the left hand as shown. Lift the end from the back of the hand up across the front and turn it around the thumb. Bend the thumb and hold the turn against the standing part of the cord. Lift the left end up around to the right. Put it over, under and over the upper center part of the knot.

Now follow the third diagram and tuck first one end and then the other end up through the center part of the knot. Lift the whole knot from the hand, turn it over, and let the ends hang down between the fingers.

It may be kept open in the design shown if used as a clothing ornament, but for a button it should be worked slowly into the second shape illustrated. Gradually ease the slack out of the various loops until it can be drawn tight.

Rope Games

The old Tug-of-War that everybody knows can be made into a game twice as interesting with two ropes instead of one. It needs four players or four teams.

Simply tie the two ropes firmly together at their centers. The four ends are then held so the ropes form an X. Since each of the players or teams will be pulling in different directions at once, it sets up tugs and balances quite different from the old Tug-of-War which was merely a contest of strength.

The game is more fun, incidentally, if everybody tries to keep up a steady pull rather than jerking on the ropes. For scoring, a circle may be drawn on the ground around all the players or a line drawn across the center.

A Jump Rope Race will provide good party amusement, especially if it has been a while since the guests last tried to jump rope. Relay teams can be set up, half the players in each team standing at opposite ends of the playing space.

Each player must give the rope a full turn over his head for every forward step he takes, the rope being passed along to the next player when the end of the space has been reached. A player may step over the rope if he can't jump, but anyone who misses has to go back and start again.

Guests paired off in couples can have fun with another party game which might be called Getting in Under the Rope. It is the reverse of jumping high hurdles in that each couple in turn must duck under a rope which is gradually lowered.

If played outdoors, two wooden rods or posts should be placed in the ground about four feet apart. They should be about five feet high. Into each of them drive eight matching sets of small and almost headless wire brads, spaced downward a half-foot apart. Measurements are approximate and need not be exact.

Fasten two metal curtain rings to a length of rope as long as the distance between the posts. Also needed are some two-foot lengths of soft cotton cord or red ribbon. If the players are wearing good clothes, an old sheet or clean mat of some kind should be placed on the ground between the posts.

The couples line up behind the posts and join hands. Their clasped hands are tied together. A bowknot may be used to tie their wrists so it will pull free quickly when the game is over. The metal rings are put over the topmost set of nails so the rope stretches across between the posts.

Moving around in a wide circle, the couples duck under the rope, two by two, and when the whole group has passed under it, the rope is lowered to the next set of nails. As it gets lower and lower, passing beneath it becomes more difficult, until finally it is necessary to crawl under the rope.

Any couple who dislodges the rope from its pegs is out of the game. Players may not touch the rope with their hands. They keep going under it in turns until all but one couple has been eliminated. The winners may be given a small prize of some kind.

Instead of posts, two trees close together or a fence post and the side of a garage wall may be used for holding the rope on its rings and pegs. Indoors, the game can be set up in a room doorway, a hallway, or at one corner of the room. If there is no place available for fastening the rope across, two people may hold the rings and lower it gradually as the others pass beneath it.

Another party game, but one which must be played in a fairly large house for the most fun, is a String Treasure Hunt. Get as many balls of string as there will be guests at the party. Each string should be several hundred feet long.

Attach a small "treasure" to one end of a string and hide it somewhere, such as in a closet, behind a couch or inside a waste basket. Then walk all over the house, letting out string from the ball as you go. Wrap the string around the back of a chair, over a door, lead it out into the hall, downstairs and back up, out through one window and in another, if the rooms are on the ground floor.

Finally lead the end of the string to some central place such as the living room and attach a tag to it with the name of one of the guests, or the names of a couple if they are going to play in teams. Then do the same with another string and a different hiding place, and so on for each player, creating a maze of strings that run all over the house.

It takes time to do, but will provide the main entertainment for a party as the players try to follow their strings and untangle them from each other. Each player may be given a stick to wind his string on as he goes along.

Circles of rope may be used in a number of games, both indoors and out. You can play a form of quoits or loop toss with them by setting up two pins for players to try to ring.

For another game, a circle of rope large enough for the hand to grip through may be thrown back and forth across a net, such as a volley ball net. The players on each side catch it and immediately toss it back, the idea being to keep it constantly in the air as in volley ball.

With a circle of rope and long wooden sticks as "lances," a form of Knight's Tournament may be played outdoors. Properly, it is played on horseback, but it is nearly as much sport afoot.

What is needed is a fairly long straightaway space. At the end of it, there should be a shoulder-high wooden post with a horizontal cross-bar that comes out to the side. This may be just a narrow strip of board nailed at a right angle to the first one.

Drive a large nail into the bottom of the cross-bar at the end farthest away from the post. With pliers, bend the nail back in an L-shape, so the head of it points directly to the rear. Hang the circle of rope on this.

The players stand back at a distance and run toward the target, holding their "lances" high. As each in turn comes abreast of the target, he plunges his stick forward and tries to put it through the small circle so as to carry the rope away on his "lance."

Circles of rope, more correctly called *Grommets,* were used by sailors for handles and as attachments to ropes and straps. Ships' cooks sometimes tied Grommets in cloth or with dish towels to wrap around dishes so as to keep food from sliding across the table during rough seas. Native dockhands in some ports put them on their heads to cushion boxes or other goods they carried balanced there while loading or unloading ship.

Here is how to make them:

Take a length of manila rope and unlay it so as to untwist one of the strands from the others. Use only that *one* strand. It should be about four times as long as the circumference of the rope circle that is desired.

Start in the middle of the strand and simply twist one part around the other, continuing to wrap it around itself in the form of a circle. Go past where you started and around the circle once again to make a three-strand Grommet. When the two ends come together, tie them with an Overhand Knot. Then tuck them under, over and under the adjoining strands of the circle as in making a splice and finally trim them off. The illustration, Plate Number 10, shows how the Grommet should look.

And, just to include all in the fun of rope games, you can give your pet dog, if you have one, some play with a rope "bone." It will be easy on his mouth and teeth and will help teach him to retrieve. Simply flatten a Grommet, wind a short length of rope tightly around it as in making a hank, and tuck in the ends. Then toss it for him to fetch.

7

Rope Magic

FOR hundreds of years, people all over the world have been
fascinated by a Jack-and-the-Beanstalk legend of a rope that
rose straight into the air and a boy who climbed it until he was
lost in the sky and vanished.

Even today, the celebrated Indian Rope Trick is the most
talked about of all the illusions of magic, but today's magicians
are unable to perform it. In fact, the great mystery of the Indian
Rope Trick is not how it was done, but whether it was ever done
at all.

Men have offered fortunes to witness a single performance
of it and some have spent much of their lives in a quest for the
truth. Learned societies have debated the issue. People of prom-
inence and high position have sworn to the accuracy of eye-
witness accounts of it. But the leading authorities of magic, those
who know every secret of the conjurer's illusions, flatly declare
that the Indian Rope Trick is impossible.

The legend already was an old one in the earliest years of
India's history. Very ancient writings, such as the *Badarayana
Vyas,* mention the rope trick. The *Vedanta Sutra,* dealing with a

period of more than thirty centuries ago, cites the trick as an example of the difference between what is make-believe and what is real: "As the magician who in reality remains upon the earth is different from the magician who with sword and shield climbs up the string."

When Marco Polo, the merchant adventurer from Venice, was exploring Asia some six hundred years ago, after the Mongol Dynasty opened safe trade routes to China, one of the wondrous events reported during his service at the court of the brilliant Emperor Kubali was the rope trick.

A Tangier-born Arabian traveler, Ibn Batuta, who visited China in the 1300's as an envoy of Sultan Muhammad Bin Tuglak, told a thrilling account of a performance at the home of a royal prince. His carefully detailed story of the supposed miracle is given in Sir Henry Yule's translation of the writings of Marco Polo.

A traveling magician made his appearance at the prince's home, according to Ibn Batuta, and was invited to show some of his marvels, "whereupon he took a wooden ball with several holes in it through which long thongs were passed and, laying hold of one of these, slung it into the air so high that we lost sight of it altogether."

Only a little of one end of a thong remained in the conjurer's hand. He called on one of the boys assisting him to mount it and the boy climbed into the sky until he went so high that Batuta and the others could no longer see him. The magician shouted to the boy, "but getting no answer, he snatched up a knife, laid hold of the thong and disappeared also." Pretty soon, Batuta said, parts of the boy's body began to fall to earth.

"Then he came down himself, all puffing and panting, and kissed the ground before the Amir and said something in Chinese," Batuta recalled. "He then took the lad's limbs, laid them together and gave them a kick, when presto, the boy got up and stood before us!"

All of this so astonished Batuta that he fainted dead away.

But the Kazi Afkharuddin, who sat next to him and didn't pass out, was somewhat cynical about the whole thing. He remarked afterwards that it was only a trick, saying, "Wallah! It is my opinion there has been neither going up nor coming down, neither marring nor amending, and all is only illusion."

However, the legend was common in many parts of China. A Chinese author, Pu Sing Ling, described a version he claimed to have seen in 1630 in which the boy, instead of vanishing, changed into a giant peach. And an English sailor of that period, Edward Milton, brought back tales of performances of the rope trick by a troupe of Chinese jugglers in the Dutch East Indies. So it even may be that the Indian Rope Trick really is Chinese.

But India claims it and it was there that the tales grew more sensational with each telling. Europeans who were stationed there or who traveled in India as visitors insisted that they saw it. Some were men of unchallenged integrity. Emperor Jehangir, who ruled in Delhi until 1627, and who was the father of the Taj Mahal builder, Shah Jehan, included an eye-witness account of the rope trick in his memoirs.

Many famous magicians, from Houdini to Maskelyne, offered large cash rewards for proof that the trick could be done, as did newspapers and various investigating societies. Some of the offers, which never were claimed, still stand. When Lord Halifax was Viceroy of India he made many attempts to see it without success. The Duke of Windsor, when he was Prince of Wales, had his agents search all of India for one performer who could show him the rope trick, but none could be found.

And yet doctors, government officials, judges, lawyers and other prominent people continued to come forward by the score and insist they had seen it or they personally knew of someone who had. Some of them gave the exact texture and diameter of the rope used, the name of the performer or of the boy who climbed it and vanished, and other details that seemed to put beyond doubt the fact that there really was an Indian Rope Trick.

They even gave explanations of the "secret" that ranged from the use of mass hypnotism to elaborate diagrams of rope-covered silken tubes inflated with some kind of lifting gas or with an inner core of bamboo joints that locked together to form a balancing pole. One of those who said he had seen the trick told how his young sister had hidden in an upstairs room to spy out the window with binoculars so as to discover a thin wire the performer had strung across between two trees the night before.

But those who argued against its possibility questioned why it supposedly always was done by poor street performers when any conjurer who actually could do it would be able to earn a fortune showing it. They doubted ancient tales that the secret was one lost to the wise men of old, since they said if such men had possessed the power, they would have used it for greater miracles and would have no need to stoop to the level of traveling entertainers.

The doubters said that any string long enough to reach into the sky to a distance where it would disappear from sight, no matter how thin it was, would have to be in a ball the size of an elephant. A rope an inch thick would have to be thousands of feet in length and a boy would need superhuman agility to climb it without knots for hand-holds.

It was believed that travelers who told about seeing the rope trick were like fishermen who exaggerated in telling about "the one that got away." Others, who might have started the story as a joke, it was said, found themselves in the position of having to defend it when the tall tale was taken seriously.

But the believers answered that there were so many nearly identical stories that they must have grown from some fact, and that the trick must have been performed somewhere. Many who claimed to be witnesses were learned men and they had no reason of personal gain for making up the story. Some admitted the strong power of suggestion in that what one person imagined he saw might be echoed by another, but they still insisted the rope trick must be true in one form or another.

In 1934, a group of magicians who served as the Occult Committee of the London Magic Circle issued a report, after careful examination of all available evidence, that denounced the Indian Rope Trick as an absolute falsehood.

"In not one single instance has any clear evidence been satisfied," the chairman declared. "The assertion that people have witnessed the temporary suspension of a great natural law at the whim of an unwashed strolling juggler is fantastic. I have no hesitation in saying that the rope trick has never been done and never will be."

The report, printed in British newspapers, aroused a storm of controversy that lasted for months. Claims and counter-claims were published around the world. The rage of arguments grew into an issue like the more recent one over the truth of flying saucers. There were interviews, investigations and letters of protest from important people who said they had been accused of lying and could prove the truth of their claims. Dozens of new "eye-witnesses" told of seeing the trick.

Finally, after its columns had been filled with the arguments for weeks, the *Times of India* attempted to settle the question by offering a large cash award for "an actual, genuine and unchallengeable performance of the Indian Rope Trick, as popularly described, before a public assemblage at Bombay."

Once again, the offer was met with silence. Although some people wrote to protest that the conditions were unfair since the trick needed to be done in surroundings of the miracle-worker's own choosing, the fact remained that there were no takers.

Leading modern magicians, who are far better equipped to produce illusions than Indian street performers, agree almost unanimously that while versions of the Indian Rope Trick can be presented on a stage, nobody can do it the way the legends tell of it.

But travelers to India and some who write about their adventures there still tell the tale of the rising rope and the vanishing boy. For many, despite all denials, the legend goes on and the mystery remains.

However, it is not the Indian Rope Trick, but another one which has brought about the present-day popularity of rope magic as a form of entertainment. It is the trick in which a length of rope apparently is cut in two and then restored to one piece again. Almost every modern magician includes some version of it in his performances.

Magicians do it with clothesline, string, ribbon, strips of paper, electric light cords and even live snakes and bicycle inner tubes. There are several hundred different ways of accomplishing the trick and the variations fill books devoted entirely to that subject alone. From it has grown a whole specialized branch of rope conjuring.

The business of pretending to cut and restore a string was an old trick even back in 1584 when its secret was first published in a now very rare book, *The Discoverie of Witchcraft* by Reginald Scot. It was the first book printed in English to explain the juggling feats of the day and one of them was how to "cut a lace asunder in the middest and to make it whole againe."

In its simplest form, it is one of the little magic puzzles most young children learn. But that fact seems only to add to its appeal when the magician presents it in a way to fool those who think they know the secret. Magicians even delight in fooling each other with new and puzzling versions of it.

The plot, as in most of the tricks which have become classics of magic, is a simple and direct one that any audience can follow. Even for those who can guess how it is done, there is fun in watching it happen. When magicians speak of "The Rope Trick," this is the one they mean.

An Australian magician, Ernest Hiskings, was among the first to develop the old string trick into a real mystery. Then Harry Kellar, the American who was considered the world's greatest magician in the period around the turn of the century, devised a new and completely baffling method. Karl Germain, another great American wizard, improved on the Kellar string trick. Dozens more had a hand in creating new versions.

But perhaps one man more than all others is responsible for today's popularity of rope magic. He is Harlan Tarbell, author and lecturer on magic, and generally considered the country's leading teacher of magic to other magicians. Tarbell substituted rope for string and thus made what had been a pocket trick, that was shown mostly for close-up amusement, into a stage illusion.

Tarbell saw his first magic show at the age of eleven and became so interested he gave a public performance of his own when he was fourteen. He started out in life as an artist, then became a doctor specializing in therapeutics, and finally turned his hobby of magic into a full-time occupation, writing, teaching and lecturing about it to groups all over the country.

During the First World War, he served with the Medical Department, attached to a balloon company, and it was while he was in Paris after the war that he became acquainted with a Hindu who started him thinking about the rope trick.

One day when they were having a deep discussion about the meaning of life, his somewhat philosophic Hindu friend said that the line of human life was like a rope, stretched between birth at one end and death at the other. If a rope were tied, the Hindu said, it would represent the circle of a man's life, which contained a knot of trouble.

Tarbell's thoughts, turning to magic from philosophy, went back to a rope mystery that Houdini had experimented with. Houdini had allowed himself to be tied to a chair, with the rope about his arms, legs and body, and had freed himself in a moment. Tarbell had learned the secret of Houdini's trick and he also re-called another one that a Chinese magician, Long Tack Sam, had performed: the throwing of a knife across the stage to sever a rope and then restore it.

Putting the two together, and adding the story about rope being the circle of life, he created a cut and restored rope mystery and dressed it up with a patter about Hindu philosophy. Tarbell first presented it in Paris. Soon newspapers were writing it up and it began to cause more comment than any magic trick in years.

Tarbell puzzled audiences around the world with it and other leading magicians found themselves completely baffled.

Houdini admitted that he was fooled and called Tarbell out of the audience at one of his shows to have him present it. Another world famous magician, Howard Thurston, stopped his own show to give Tarbell and the rope trick a place on his stage. Magicians everywhere realized the appeal that rope magic had and they began devising their own rope tricks. Tarbell was offered large sums of money for his secret, which he finally released to other performers.

"Even though I had worked out an effective cut and restored mystery, there wasn't anything new in the method," he modestly wrote later. "I had just taken an old principle and given it a new treatment."

Meanwhile, a boy who was to become probably the best known magician in America today, Milbourne Christopher, had his own interest in magic started by the old cut and restored string trick. It was the first trick he ever saw. His father showed it to him in his home in Baltimore when he was six years old and it so intrigued him that he never forgot it.

As he began to grow up and became a Boy Scout, ropes and knots held a fascination for him almost as strong as his hobby of magic. He read all the books about knots that he could find. Washington was close enough to Baltimore for a teen-ager to visit easily, and he soon began making the trip regularly, not to see the sights of the capital, but to dig into the maze of anthropological files in the Library of Congress about the primitive uses of rope.

During a regional convention of the International Brotherhood of Magicians at Lancaster, Pennsylvania, Christopher was among the young performers who entered a contest to present original tricks. He displayed a piece of rope that was about three feet long. Christopher handled it freely to show that it was unprepared. Then, casually pulling it between his hands, he visibly stretched it to four times its original length. His trick won him a prize and the acclaim of other magicians.

When he went to Europe in 1936, to appear as a performer with the pantomimic comedian, Fred Sanborn, he worked out a complete routine with rope. It was easy to carry and yet showed up against his black dinner jacket in the largest of theaters. Audiences seemed to enjoy watching his interesting manipulations with something they were familiar with in everyday life.

It was a time when specialty acts were gaining great theatrical popularity. There were magicians who did tricks with nothing but watches and clocks, others who performed only with coins, silk handkerchiefs, cards or cigarettes. "I had never heard of a rope specialist," Christopher said, "so I tried to work out something new."

He also recalled being on the same program with an illusionist who had several huge trunks filled with equipment. It took the illusionist three hours to set up his act before the show and another two hours to pack it away afterwards. Christopher walked out with his rope, did his act, folded up the rope and put it in his pocket, and that was that.

Christopher's rope specialty caught on and he became a headliner, featured in the shows in which he appeared. His rope magic took him to thirty-six countries, put him in top theaters and in night clubs. He turned again to other forms of magic, including big illusions, for his own full-evening show on Broadway and for the many nationwide television shows he has given.

But on his own programs or when he is a featured guest on others, he often shows rope tricks rather than some of his bigger mysteries. They still hold the same fascination, not only for Christopher, but also for those who watch the seemingly unbelievable things he can do with a piece of rope.

He was once challenged by a skeptical newspaper reporter to do a ten-minute sleight-of-hand act without using his sleeves or his pockets. The reporter was a believer in the common rumor that magicians sneak everything into their pockets or up their sleeves. Christopher took up the challenge.

"It was easy with a few pieces of rope," he said. "I put on the act wearing a bathing suit."

A ROPE MAGIC SHOW

MAGICIANS usually do their rope tricks with very soft, hollow-braided white cotton clothesline. It should be unglazed and have no chemical stiffening treatment. If you shop around in the variety stores, you should find the kind best suited to rope magic.

However, many of these tricks can be done with any ordinary white cotton clothesline if it is worked until it becomes soft and pliable. Some can be performed with string or ribbon, which is easy to carry around in the pocket, so you can show your rope magic wherever you happen to be.

At the end of the chapter, you will find two suggested routines, one impromptu and the other for a set-up act. All the tricks can be performed separately, of course, or you can make up your own act from them.

Talk to go with the tricks has been suggested, but you should put it into your own words. Keep the secrets to yourself, because to reveal them only spoils everybody's fun. Practice in front of a mirror until you know what you are doing so well that you don't have to think about what to do next.

And never repeat a trick for the same audience since with the surprise of it gone, they probably will catch on. Surprise is the most important element of magic. Try to keep people guessing as to exactly what is going to happen next.

THREAD TO ROPE

How It Looks:

You show a spool of white thread and both hands appear otherwise empty. Breaking off a length of thread, you discard the spool. You start winding the thread into a small ball in your left hand as you talk about how easily thread may become snarled and tangled.

"But a way to keep that from happening," you say, "is simply to make the thread bigger." With a magic wave of your hand, you reach into your left fist and, instead of the thread, draw out a length of rope. You display your empty hands and remark, "This way, it always comes out straight."

What You Need:

A 100-yard spool of Number 8 white cotton thread.

A needle.

A four-foot length of soft hollow-braided white cotton clothes-line with the center core removed. To remove the core, push back the outer braiding a little, grip the core, and gradually strip it free by working the outer braiding down on it a few inches at a time. This will give you a rope that can be folded into a very small space.

How You Fix It:

Place one end of the rope on your left palm and fold the rest of the rope against itself, accordion-fashion, in one-inch pleats until all but about four inches of it is folded. Wind the remaining end of rope tightly around the folds and then make a tiny loop and tuck it in under so it holds.

Now unwind a little of the thread from the spool, but don't break it off. Thread the needle with it and draw the thread once through the end of the rope. Pull the thread out a bit and remove the needle.

The wooden rim of the spool has a small notch, put there by the manufacturers to hold the thread as it is used. Draw the part of the thread that comes from the spool and the end of it that goes through the rope together. Bring them up to the bottom of the spool and hook both threads in that notch at its rim. Trim off the excess thread, but not too closely.

You now should have a spool of thread with the folded rope

hanging beneath it on the loop of thread as illustrated in Plate Number 11. Have this in the pocket of your jacket or concealed in a small sewing basket on your table.

What You Do:

Casually show both hands empty. Reach to your pocket or to the basket with your right hand and take the spool of thread between your thumb and forefinger. Bring out your hand with its back toward the audience, the right fingers partly closed in a natural manner, and so that most of the spool shows above the top of the hand. The rope will hang hidden within your fingers. There is no need to hold it.

Again, show your left hand empty. Reach with the left hand to the right so the left thumb and forefinger can take the spool, the back of the left hand toward the audience. This automatically transfers the rope to the concealment of the left fingers.

Casually show the right hand empty. Bring the hands together. Grip the end of the thread with the left fingers, keeping the rope concealed, and unhook it from the spool. Immediately draw the spool to the right, unreeling a length of thread. Break it off, discard the spool, and gather the thread into your left hand with the help of your right hand.

As you wad the thread into a tiny ball, pull it free from the rope. Push the balled thread with your right fingers down into the crotch between your left first and second fingers and leave it there.

Pull out the rope and display it. With the thread concealed between the fingers, both hands may be shown empty. Get rid of the little ball of thread as you put the spool back into the basket or into your pocket.

QUICK AND EASY CUT ROPE

How It Looks:

You tie a knot in the center of a length of rope or show a rope in which a knot has been left tied from some previous trick.

Reaching into your jacket pocket, you take out a small pair of scissors. You pull up the center of the rope and cut right through it at both sides of the knot, letting the knot drop to the floor. You then trim the ends so that everyone may be sure the rope really has been cut.

Without any false moves, you flip the rope into the air by one end and it is fully restored. The knot is still tied in the center of it.

What You Need:

A four-foot length of rope.
A four-inch piece of rope.
White thread.
A pair of sharp scissors small enough to fit in your pocket.

How You Fix It:

Tie an Overhand Knot in the small piece of rope and bring the two ends together. Wrap several turns of white thread around them and tie the thread to hold them. You should now have a small loop of rope with a knot in the center. Place this in your left jacket pocket with the loop pointing forward. Put the scissors in the same pocket, handles to the front.

What You Do:

Show the long rope and tie a knot in its center. Double it and hold it with your right hand so the middle of the rope where the knot is shows above your hand. The two ends of rope should hang down inside your palm. (See Plate Number 11.)

With your left hand, reach into your pocket. Take the scissors in your hand so the blades are against your fingers and the handles to the front of them. Now close your fingers around the extra loop so it is completely concealed within the same hand. It should lie against the blade of the scissors. You will have to practice this so there will be no delay. It should look as though you merely were removing the scissors from your pocket.

Bring out the scissors. Move the right hand, which holds the rope, over to the left. Place the real knot into your left palm directly on top of the fake one concealed there. Take the handle of the scissors with your right hand and lift them free of your left hand. Now pull the fake loop and knot into view above your left hand. All of this should be done easily and naturally, as though you were just transferring the scissors to your right hand so as to cut with them.

Cut through the fake loop at one side of the knot and then at the other side, slowly and deliberately. Let the cut-away knot fall to the floor. Cut off another piece of the small extra loop. Then bring the scissors over as if to cut again, but instead, nip the remaining end of the loop with the blade of the scissors and let that drop to the floor with the rest of the pieces. Now take one end of the rope and flip it into the air so it appears fully restored with the knot still in it.

THE FISHING COWBOY

How It Looks:

You show a length of rope and snap out the end of it from your hand several times while you tell about a dude ranch where all the guests were fishing a stream with expensive rods and reels. "One of the ranch cowboys came along and watched the dudes for a few minutes," you say. "Then he just took his rope, tossed it at the water, and lassoed himself a fish—cowboy style."

As you say the last words, an imitation fish appears tied at the end of the snapping rope.

What You Need:

A four-foot length of rope.

A rubber or plastic fish of a kind that may be concealed in the palm of your hand. There are many different types of these on sale at dime store toy counters and in toy stores. Look around until you find one that will do. If nothing else, you can cut one

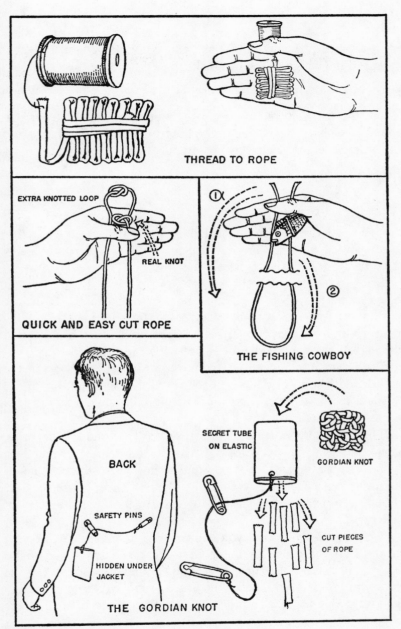

THREAD TO ROPE

EXTRA KNOTTED LOOP

REAL KNOT

QUICK AND EASY CUT ROPE

① ②

THE FISHING COWBOY

BACK

SAFETY PINS

HIDDEN UNDER JACKET

SECRET TUBE ON ELASTIC

GORDIAN KNOT

CUT PIECES OF ROPE

THE GORDIAN KNOT

PLATE Nº 11

from a piece of heavy cardboard and color it, or whittle a raw carrot in the rough shape of a fish.

How You Fix It:

Tie the fish tightly to the rope about three inches from one end. Place the rope behind something on a table or, if you use this as an opening trick, have it in your hands as you enter.

What You Do:

Hold the end of the rope to which the fish is tied under the crotch of your right thumb, with the back of your hand to the audience so the fish is concealed in the palm of it. Hold the other end of the rope in your left hand. Show the rope loosely stretched in front of you. (See Plate Number 11.)

Bring the left end of the rope to the right hand. Grip it between the tip of your right first finger and thumb. Drop the left hand to your side. Turn your body slightly to the left. Give your right hand an outward and downward flick and release the end of the rope which does not have the fish tied to it.

Do this as if you were just giving the rope a little snap in the air. Bring the end of the rope back up to the right hand with the left and repeat the same move of snapping it out. Do this several times as you tell the story.

The last time, instead of releasing the free end of the rope, keep that gripped by your right hand and release the end to which the fish is tied. Do it without hesitation, so there seems to be no difference in what you do. To the audience, it will seem as though the fish suddenly was caught from the air at the end of the rope.

With a different story, you can make a handkerchief, playing card, or anything else small enough to be concealed in your hand appear at the end of the rope. Or you can have a knot tied in the rope, conceal it as you would the fish, and make it seem as though you were able to tie a knot just by snapping it into the end of the rope.

THE GORDIAN KNOT

How It Looks:

You tell the story about the magic knot tied by Gordius that nobody could untie and show a large knot that is a seeming mass of twists and turns without beginning or end.

Pushing it down into your left fist, you explain how the knot defied all attempts to unbind it until Alexander the Great came along. (For background that will help you make up patter for the trick, refer to the legend of the Gordian Knot in Chapter Three.)

Tell how he slashed it apart with a mighty stroke of his sword and demonstrate by chopping at your left hand with your right. Slowly opening the fingers of your left hand, you say, "And this is what happened to the magic knot of Gordius." From your hand, as though severed by a sword, spill a shower of cut pieces of rope instead of the tangled knot. There is nothing else in your hands.

What You Need:

A three-foot length of rope.
Eight pieces of rope, each about two inches long.
A spool of white thread.
A three-foot length of black cord elastic.
The cardboard from the center of a roll of paper kitchen towels.
Two small safety pins.
A pair of scissors.
To perform this trick, you must wear a jacket.

How You Fix It:

First, with the long piece of rope, make an imitation of the Gordian Knot. Tie it in a mass of big-looped knots. Bind the two ends tightly together with thread and tie a knot around them so the ends will be lost in the center of it.

Now cut a piece off the cardboard tube two inches long. Flatten it and poke a small hole through one side about one-quarter inch from the end. Thread one end of the elastic cord through this and knot it there tightly. Tie the other end of the elastic through the end hole of one of the safety pins.

Attach that safety pin above your right hip. Run the cord elastic through the other safety pin and fasten that one at your left hip. The elastic should run across your back with the flat paper tube drawn against the safety pin that is at your left side. Your jacket, when you put it on, will cover the whole arrangement. To try the pull, hold the paper tube concealed in your left hand, release your fingers, and it will fly back out of sight under your jacket. (See Plate Number 11.)

Prepare for the trick by stuffing the short lengths of rope into the flattened tube. Jam them in so they will stay secure. Have the Gordian Knot on your table.

What You Do:

If the trick is being shown by itself, so that your hands need not be free during previous tricks, you can start with the loaded tube already in your left hand and the knot held by the fingers of the same hand. Otherwise, you will have to get the tube secretly into your left hand by means of the ruse about to be explained.

Start by showing the Gordian Knot and telling its story. While you are pulling it through your fingers to display it, "accidentally" drop the knot to the floor a little to the front of you and to the left. Turn your right side to the audience as you lean down to pick up the knot. At the same moment, secretly swing back your left hand, grasp the tube, and conceal it within your left fingers. Lift your partly closed left hand up in front of your waist.

Bring the knot immediately to the left hand and start stuffing it into your fist. Actually, jam it tightly into the top end of the tube, secretly pushing the cut pieces out into your fist from the bottom of the tube.

Release the tube to let it fly to concealment beneath your

jacket. Finish the story about Alexander the Great and his sword and slowly open your left hand to let the pieces shower to the floor, casually showing that both hands are otherwise empty.

SYMPATHETIC ROPES

How It Looks:

You count four separate lengths of rope from one hand to the other. Bunching up two of the ropes, you put them aside. The other two, you tie together with a firm knot. You then pretend to pluck the knot by magic from those two and pass it to the first pair.

When you shake out the ropes, the two that were tied together have come apart and the two previously separate ropes are now tightly tied together.

What You Need:

Four lengths of rope, each about four feet long.

How You Fix It:

Tie a very loose, wide-open Overhand Knot in one of the ropes about two inches from the top end. The open loop of the knot should be about one and one-half inches across, but the whole knot should be small enough to be concealed by the palm of the hand when the end of the rope is gripped under the right thumb.

Place the other three ropes with that one, their ends even at the top so that all four may be picked up at one time. Put them in a basket or behind something on the table.

What You Do:

Pick up the four ropes together with the right hand, the back of the hand to the audience and the secret knot hanging concealed inside the palm, the long ends of the rope hanging down. (See Plate Number 12.)

Bring the left hand over the *front* of the right. Grip the end of the first rope, which has the hidden knot in it, under the left thumb. Without moving the left hand, draw the right hand down away from it, transferring the rope to the left hand so the knot will be hidden within the left palm. Count aloud, "One."

Bring the right hand back toward the left. Put the end of the second rope between the third and little fingers at the *bottom* of the left hand to hold it. The end should stick up between the fingers and inside the left palm so that it is just at the edge of the loop of the concealed knot. But don't pull it through yet. Leave the second rope in that position in the left hand and draw the right hand down and away. Count aloud, "Two."

Now bring the right hand over again as though you were about to take the third rope with the left, but pause an instant. Reach with your right fingers to the end of the second rope that is already in your left hand and draw it up through the knot to bring the end to the top of the left hand next to the first rope. This should look as if you are adjusting the position of the two ropes and not as though you were threading one through the knot of the other.

Immediately now, place the next rope from the right hand beside the others in the left hand and count aloud, "Three." Then add the fourth and count, "Four."

Leave them there a minute as you drop your right hand to your side. Say, "Four separate pieces of rope." Bring your right hand up and give all four a little tug at the top and again at the bottom, as though displaying them, but really pulling the knot tight.

Take away the last two ropes with the right hand and drop them to the table for a moment. Bunch up the two that are secretly knotted and place them on a chair or at the other side of the table. Say, "We'll put these two over here."

Now, tie the other two together with the Fake Square Knot described in Chapter Four as you say, "And we'll tie these two together." Bunch them up and put them at a distance from the others.

All that remains to be done is to act out the pantomime of passing the knot from one set to the other. Shake out the two that you tied and they will fall apart. Lift the other pair and show that they have become knotted by magic.

BAG OF ROPE

How It Looks:

You show an empty plastic bag and place both hands inside it. Turning the bag from one side to the other, you let the audience see that your hands are empty. You rub your hands together and gradually a rope appears between them inside the bag.

What You Need:

A plastic bag that is as wide as the span of both of your hands together when your fingers are spread far apart. This should be the clear, not smoky-colored, type of plastic. If you can't find one, a net cord bag of the kind in which oranges often are sold will do.

A five-foot length of rope with the core removed. If you prefer, the core may be left in, but a shorter length should then be used.

How You Fix It:

Place one end of the rope on your left palm and fold the rope upon itself in one-inch pleats, accordion-fashion, as for the *Thread to Rope* trick, winding the last few inches around the folds and tucking in a loop of the end to hold it. But this time, leave a good inch of the end sticking up from the small bundle that you have made of the rope.

What You Do:

If this is to be used as an opening trick, grip the very end of the rope in the crotch of the right thumb so the rope hangs concealed inside the palm of your hand when the back of the hand is toward the audience. Hold the plastic bag at the fingertips of the same hand. Enter holding it that way.

However, if you want to do this later in your routine, have the plastic bag and the little bundle of rope in a basket or behind something on your table. Place it so the end stands straight up. When you are ready to perform the trick, reach for the plastic bag with your right hand and secretly grip the end of the rope under your thumb to hold it as described above.

Take the plastic bag from your right hand with your left thumb and forefinger holding it open at the top. With the back of your right hand still toward the audience and concealing the rope within its palm, thrust your right hand inside to the bottom of the bag. Hold the bag out away from you to your left.

Now place your left hand into the bag, *palm facing front,* directly above the right hand. With your right hand, press the concealed rope against the rear of the bag that is away from the audience. Open wide the fingers of both hands. Your right palm keeps the rope hidden. (See Plate Number 12.)

Hold your hands that way a moment so the audience has a clear view of them inside the bag. Now swing your whole body around to your right with your hands still outstretched inside the bag. As you do so, lift your right hand up to the top of the bag and thrust your left hand to the bottom. Your palms pass across each other inside the bag as you reverse the position of your hands straight up and down.

This move will take practice before the mirror, but if it is properly timed, the swing of your body will hide the changing concealment of the rope, which merely stays at the bottom of the bag so that the left palm now covers it instead of the right.

At this point, you should be standing with your left side to the audience, the bag held out to your right and the rope hidden by your left palm against the side of the bag as it originally was by your right palm. Cup both hands together and work the bundle loose with your thumbs, shaking the bag up and down slightly to let the rope gradually spill out into view inside it.

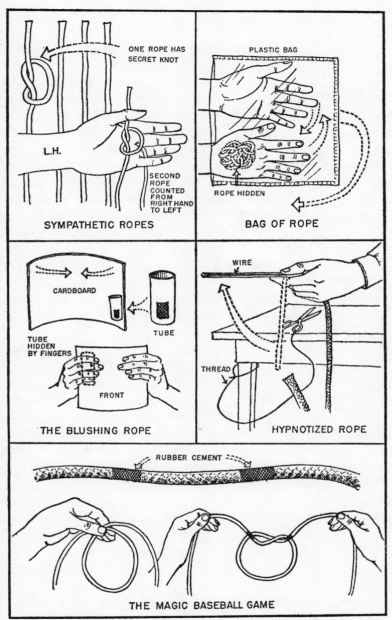

SYMPATHETIC ROPES

ONE ROPE HAS SECRET KNOT

L.H.

SECOND ROPE COUNTED FROM RIGHT HAND TO LEFT

BAG OF ROPE

PLASTIC BAG

ROPE HIDDEN

THE BLUSHING ROPE

CARDBOARD

TUBE

TUBE HIDDEN BY FINGERS

FRONT

HYPNOTIZED ROPE

WIRE

THREAD

THE MAGIC BASEBALL GAME

RUBBER CEMENT

PLATE Nº 12

ROPES FROM THE AIR

How It Looks:

You reach out with your right hand as if to pluck some invisible object from the air. Failing to catch anything, you appear momentarily puzzled, but you try again, making a grab at the air with the left hand. A rope appears at your fingertips.

Drawing the rope through your hands to show that it is a single rope and that your hands are otherwise empty, you run your fingers down the length of it several times and the one rope multiplies itself by some sudden magic and becomes two ropes.

What You Need:

Two four-foot lengths of rope with the cores removed.
Two hairpins.
Two small safety pins.
A jacket must be worn to do the trick.

How You Fix It:

Fold each rope into a small pleated bundle in the manner described for the *Bag of Rope* or the *Thread to Rope.* Thrust the prongs of one of the hairpins deeply into the center of each bundle so that it holds firmly and only the round part at the top of the hairpin sticks out. Put a safety pin through each of the hairpins.

Put on your jacket and fasten one of the safety pins to the *underside* of your jacket at the edge just over your right hip. The hidden bundle of rope should hang suspended by the safety pin and hairpin so that it is just above the edge of the jacket, in a position where your fingers can curl under and reach it when your hand falls naturally to your side. Attach the second small bundle of rope in a similar position at your left side.

What You Do:

Casually show both hands empty. Turn your body to the left, so its right side is toward the audience. With your right hand, reach high into the air as if to catch something. This covers a secret move to be made with your left hand, which you have dropped naturally to your left side. Reach beneath the edge of your jacket with your left hand and draw the rope off its holder so it falls into your fingers. Grasp the very end that sticks up from the bundle in the crotch of your left first and second fingers.

Now, let your right hand fall to your side. Face front a moment with the rope concealed by your left fingers as that hand also hangs at your side. Don't contract your hand or make any attempt to "palm" the rope. There is no need to squeeze your fingers tight, since the end clipped high between them will keep the hidden rope in position.

Turn your body to the right, so your left side is toward the audience. Reach high into the air with your left hand. Keeping a tight grip on the end of the rope that is between your left fingers, push down on the bundle with your thumb and it will fall apart, revealing the rope as it appears hanging from your fingertips.

While you are doing this with your left hand, your right hand takes the opportunity to steal the second bundle of rope secretly from under the right side of your jacket. Face forward, keeping the second rope concealed in your right hand. Hold up the visible rope with the left hand, palm facing front so that everyone may see there is nothing else in that hand.

Now turn your left palm in towards yourself and bring it down opposite your waist. Bring your right hand over to your left so that the tip of your right little finger rests along the knuckles of the first finger of the left hand. Let the concealed ball of rope drop from your right hand into your left during the instant that your two hands are brought together.

With your right hand thumb and first finger, nip the end of the visible rope and draw it up away from the left hand, running the left hand down it almost to the bottom end. Turn the palm of your right hand outwards to show that it is empty except for the top end of the visible rope that it is holding.

Drop that held end from your right hand. Lift your left hand a little. With your right hand, reach down beneath the left hand and grasp the short end of the visible rope. Draw that down through the left hand. Drop the end of the rope from your right hand.

Now hold the left hand high and keep a tight grip with it on both the visible rope and the end of the hidden bundle. Reach up with the right hand and pull down on the hidden rope, running your right hand straight down along the visible rope to the bottom. As you do, the second rope will appear beside the first one.

HYPNOTIZED ROPE

How It Looks:

You pick up a short length of rope and a pair of scissors from your table. Doubling the rope in your left hand, you bring the scissors up as if to cut one end of it. The end of the rope flips itself into the air, as though springing away from the scissors. You look surprised and try again. The rope jumps again.

Dropping the scissors into the breast pocket of your jacket, you remark that you have heard of people being hypnotized, but never rope. You pass your hand over the end of the rope and it stands up straight. Then you take both hands away and the rope floats by itself in mid-air.

Catching the rope, you take out the scissors and make another swipe at cutting it. Again, the rope seems to jump away. You coil up the rope and drop it to the table with the scissors. Shaking your head, you shrug and remark, "Isn't that the strangest thing?"

What You Need:

A four-foot length of rope with the core removed.

Two feet of medium-sized aluminum wire.

A spool of white cotton thread, a spool of black nylon thread, and a needle.

A pair of scissors.

A table.

This must be performed at a distance of at least eight feet from those watching. If possible, you should be wearing dark clothes.

How You Fix It:

With the core removed, slide the aluminum wire down inside the rope where the core was. Take the needle and white thread and sew the top end of the rope closed. Slide the wire up inside it and sew the rope across the center beneath the bottom end of the wire. This leaves the wire in a pocket at the top end of the rope. (See Plate Number 12.)

Thread the needle with a four-foot length of black thread and pass it through the rope two inches from the top. Remove the needle and tie that end of the black thread to the rear left leg of the table near its top. Tie the other end of the thread to the handle of the scissors. Stretch out the thread and bring the rope to the middle of it.

Put the scissors and rope on the table and leave them there until you are ready to perform the trick. Then pick up the un-wired end of rope with your left hand. With the help of your right hand, pull it back through your left hand until your left fingers touch the wire. Drop the rope from your right hand.

It should now hang down from the left hand by its center, the unwired part to the left and the wired half to the right. The end of the wire at the center of the rope should come directly between the left thumb and forefinger.

Move a little to the left of the table. Pick up the scissors with your right hand and bring them up as if to cut a piece from the wired side of the rope. By pressing the left thumb down on the wire which is beneath it, you can make that half of the rope jump up to the right, away from the scissors. Just give it a tiny flick with your thumb as you clip at the air with the scissors. Release the pressure of your thumb and let the rope fall back immediately. Do the same thing again.

Now drop the scissors into your breast pocket. With your right hand, make a pretended hypnotic pass over the rope. Press down firmly with the left thumb so the wired end stands straight out. Turn the left hand and bring the rigid end up so it is vertical. Move away from the table a little more, until you feel the black thread draw taut between you and the table.

Slowly remove both hands and the rope will remain suspended on the invisible thread. Make a few passes over the top of it and around the sides, being careful not to touch the thread.

Catch the center of the rope with your left hand. Get the wire under your thumb and lift your left hand high. Remove the scissors from your pocket with your right hand. Make another swipe with the scissors and jump the rope away from them, moving close to the table again as you do this.

Now simply coil up the rope around your left hand, starting with the wired end, just as though you were coiling any other rope. The wire will bend easily. Drop the coiled rope and scissors to the table.

The wire may be straightened out again so that the prepared rope will serve for many performances.

THE BLUSHING ROPE

How It Looks:

"This is a very bashful rope," you say, holding up a length of rope for everyone to see. "It hates to perform in public. But I would like to have it show you how intelligent it is about untying knots." You tie a knot in the center of it. Speaking of the rope, you say, "Go ahead, now. Untie yourself. Show everybody how smart you are." But nothing happens and you shake your head. "As I said, it's a bashful one. Perhaps we should give it a little privacy."

You show a piece of red cardboard, roll it into a tube, and stuff the rope inside it. Peeking into the top, you say, "Yes, it's freeing itself now from the knot." You reach to the bottom end of the tube and pull out the rope. The knot has gone, as you promised, but the white rope has changed to a fiery red.

Showing the tube otherwise empty, you hold up the red rope and say, "I told you it was bashful. It's blushing all over."

What You Need:

A three-foot length of white rope, with the core removed.
Another three-foot length, core removed, that has been dyed red. This may be done with ordinary textile dye.
Glue or rubber cement.
A length of one-inch wide red ribbon.
A tube of red cardboard made as follows:
Get a sheet of red poster board from a stationery store. Cut a piece 8" by 15". With the long edge at the bottom, measure off six inches from the right. Come up two inches from the bottom and put a pencil dot there. Use a pair of scissors or a razor blade in a holder and cut down in a straight line from the top of the cardboard to the pencil dot. Then cut from the dot all the way across to the right. Remove the cut-away section.

This two-inch wide tab at the right is to be made into a small tube. Roll the right end of the tab in upon itself for a distance of about one inch. Coat it with glue or rubber cement and roll it to the left, sticking it tight. Continue this until you have the small tube firmly stuck to the bottom right corner of the larger cardboard of which it is a part. (See Plate Number 12.)

Now cut two little slits at the center sides of this small tube so you may thread the ribbon through. It should go right across the inside center of the small tube to divide it into two compartments. Poke your finger into the tube and gently press the ribbon down to the bottom of it. Glue the ends of the ribbon to the outside of the tube to hold them and trim away any excess ribbon. You can fasten the ribbon with Scotch tape if you prefer.

Let it all dry thoroughly and then roll the larger cardboard around the small tube. Roll it tightly with the small tube inside and run your hands around the outside a number of times until the larger cardboard curls by itself, so that when its sides are released they tend to spring inward naturally.

When you are ready to set it up for the trick, push the ribbon to the bottom of the little tube and tuck the red rope inside it from the top, squeezing it in until it holds tightly. Have the partly rolled cardboard on your table, with the tube end to the right at the rear, and the white rope beside it.

What You Do:

Follow the plot of the trick as given. Show the white rope and tie a knot in it. Go through the by-play of waiting for it to untie itself. Put down the rope. Pick up the cardboard with your right hand so that your fingers curl around the small tube and conceal it. Bring it up vertically toward the left. With your left hand, uncurl the other edge of the cardboard toward the left.

Hold it up between your hands, the right fingers hiding the small tube beneath them. It should look as though that hand is just helping to hold the cardboard open so everybody can see that it is empty. Remove your left hand entirely. The piece of cardboard should spring by itself partly around the right fingers. Turn it slightly more to the right and roll the cardboard into a large tube around the smaller one.

Now, still holding the rolled cardboard vertically, tuck the white rope up into the end where the small tube is. As you do, the red rope will be pushed out and the white will take its place. Make sure the white rope is tucked in tightly. Draw the red rope out the other end of the cardboard and comment on how it is blushing all over.

Put your right-hand fingers around the small tube to conceal it as you did when you first showed the cardboard empty. Pull the cardboard open with your left hand to show it apparently still empty. Remove your left hand and let the cardboard snap back by itself into a roll and put it aside.

THE MAGIC BASEBALL GAME

How It Looks:

"I'd like to show you what I call a magic game of baseball," you say as you display a length of rope and then coil it around your left hand. "Instead of a ball, we'll use this rope. And instead of three bases, this game has only one—a paper bag." With your right hand, you pick up a paper bag, show it empty, and drop the coiled rope inside. You put the bag on your table.

"Now we need some players for our team," you say, as you pick up a second length of rope and show it. "Are there any ball players in the audience? Please raise your hands." As you speak, you tie a large Overhand Knot in the second rope and hold the rope outstretched by its two ends so that all may see the knot. "How about you?" You nod to someone in the audience. "Will you be our catcher? Just hold up your hands as though you were going to catch a ball and I'll throw you this knot."

You flick the rope forward, still holding both ends, and the knot visibly vanishes. "Did you catch it?" you ask. "Good—just hold it for a minute. Now we need a pitcher for our team." You tie a second knot in the center of the rope and nod to someone else. "Will you be our pitcher? Hold up your hands and I'll throw you this one." Again you make a knot vanish as if throwing it in his direction.

"And now, a shortstop." As the third person holds up his hands to catch an invisible knot, you add to the comedy by saying, "Oh, I'm sorry. You dropped it. Would you mind picking it up? It fell next to your chair. Right down there."

You now put aside that rope and pick up the paper bag containing the first coiled-up rope. Turning toward the first person who is supposed to be holding an invisible knot, you say, "Would you please throw yours back?" As he makes the motion, you move the bag as though catching it and the sound of the knot landing inside the bag is heard. You do the same with the other two players, "catching" the knots in the bag as they are thrown.

"Now, let's see how you've done," you say. Lifting out the original rope, you show that three knots have become tied in it. You throw aside the paper bag. "Say—you're pretty good ball players!"

What You Need:

Two five-foot lengths of rope.
A bottle of rubber cement.
A paper bag.

How You Fix It:

The first rope, the one that will be coiled up and put in the paper bag, needs no preparation. But the second rope, from which the knots visibly disappear, has to be fixed with two patches of rubber cement. (See Plate Number 12.)

Find the center of the rope and slide your fingers down about four inches to each side. That is where the two spots of cement should go. Coat the rope with one-inch circles of cement in those two places. Make a band of it right around the rope and put it on heavily so it really soaks in. Let it dry thoroughly and give it a second heavy coating in those places. Then let it dry again before you use the rope.

Put the prepared rope on the table with the paper bag on top of it and the unprepared rope on top of that.

What You Do:

This really is a small act in itself and the fun of it depends on the audience taking part in the make-believe ball game. The magic should be practiced first, step-by-step, until you have it down perfectly. Then the act should be rehearsed as you would study a part for a play.

Since the plot of the trick has been given in detail so you can follow it easily, we will deal here only with the actual moves that are made.

The unprepared rope is shown and coiled three times on the left hand to make three knots secretly as explained for Any Number of Knots in Chapter Four. But there is one small difference. After you have made the coils on the left hand, don't pull the end of the rope up through them right away. Hold the coils in the left hand and pick up the paper bag from the table with the right hand. Shake out the bag and show it empty.

Now, as you are asking whether there are any ball players in the audience, pull the end up through the coils. Hold the end and put the rope in the bag, but keep the end pressed against the inside top of the bag with your fingers as you put the bag on the table.

The delay in pulling the end up through the coils makes the move less suspicious, so it looks as though you are just coiling up the rope. And keeping the end of the rope at the top of the bag will avoid fumbling for it later.

Next, take up the prepared rope, holding it with both hands near the center. Both hands should be palm down, with the rope held between the respective thumb and first two fingers of each hand. Casually slide your hands apart along the rope a little until you feel the rough spots of rubber cement come into your fingers.

Holding the two spots of cement, move the right hand forward toward the audience and then over to the left to form a loop in the rope that brings the spots of cement together. Give them a little squeeze with your left thumb and finger so they stick tightly.

Slide the right thumb and finger along the rope towards the right end of it. Put that end through the loop, from the front, pointing towards yourself, just as if you were tying a knot. Gently slide both hands out to the ends of the rope and the fake knot will hold in the center. But if you give the rope a quick forward jerk, the knot will vanish instantly.

Throw the three knots to the persons supposed to catch them, one to the right, a second in the center, and the third to someone on the left. Put aside that rope. Pick up the paper bag with your right hand. Your second finger goes inside the bag and holds the end of the rope against the top rear of the bag. The other fingers of the right hand remain on the outside at the rear of the bag.

As the players throw their knots back, one at a time, make the sound of them landing in the bag by snapping your right first finger against the bag with the help of your thumb. Transfer the bag to your left hand, holding the end of the rope inside the top with your left fingers. Reach into the bag with your right hand. Take the end of the rope and give it a few shakes inside the bag as you remove it so that the knots will fall into place along it. Hold the rope high to show that the three invisible knots have been "caught."

TWO ROPE MAGIC ACTS

YOUR ROUTINE of rope tricks should start with something quick and surprising, then offer a brief display of your skill with rope, go on to something puzzling, next put in a little comedy, and then end with your best trick.

But no rope magic is any good, no matter what the effect is meant to be, unless *you* can do it well. Probably you will find some of these tricks come to you more easily than others. Choose the ones you are confident about doing. It is far better to do a simple trick entertainingly than to attempt an elaborate one that fails.

Don't try to include everything in one performance. A routine that lasts six to ten minutes should be enough. Plan it and practice it and then don't be tempted to add to it on the spur of the moment. Do only what you have carefully rehearsed.

Here are two suggested routines, one for a show when you can set your things up in advance, and the other for a so-called "impromptu" performance, when you have no chance to arrange the set-up of your props. However, even for the "impromptu" show, you will need to fix your ropes ahead of time, so they may be carried in your pockets or in a briefcase.

Act One (*for the set-up show*):

Thread To Rope.

Tricky Knots (See Chapter Four)—The Lightning Knot; Shoulder Knot; Vanishing Overhand Knot; Wrist Loop; Slide Off Knot; Speedy Bowknot; Vanishing Bowknot; The Instant One-handed Knot; Slide Off Knot again; One-Handed Ring Hitch, shown first as a monocle and then eyeglasses; The Lightning Knot again, to leave a knot in the center of the rope.

Quick And Easy Cut Rope.

The Blushing Rope.

Ropes From The Air.

The Gordian Knot.

Hypnotized Rope.

The Magic Baseball Game.

Act Two (*for the impromptu show*):

Bag Of Rope.

Tricky Knots as before, adding The Bachelor's Needle; Chefalo Knot; Any Number of Knots and String of Vanishing Knots, if desired, ending again with a Lightning Knot.

Quick And Easy Cut Rope.

The Fishing Cowboy.

Sympathetic Ropes. (Cut the fish from the end of the second rope to use for this, along with the first rope you have been using. Then pick up the two additional ropes, including the one with the concealed knot.)

The Gordian Knot.

Making Up Other Tricks

With the methods given here, you should be able to make up some unusual rope tricks of your own. A little twist to the story will produce a brand-new effect. Go back through the book and pick out some of the stories, legends and facts about rope that interest you and then make up magic to illustrate them.

The little cardboard tube on the elastic that was used in the Gordian Knot trick, for instance, will change rope into almost anything the same size or make a rope disappear. With your knowledge of Tricky Knots and the visibly vanishing one in The Magic Baseball Game, you might make up a magic story about sailors or the witches who used to sell knots to hold the wind.

A wired rope such as that used in the Hynotized Rope trick might be tied in the shape of a small lariat to be spun around and then float away off the stage by itself. Instead of using the cardboard tube to change a white rope to red as in The Blushing Rope, you might change it to a metal chain or roll of imitation money. With just a piece of rope and your imagination, you can make up dozens of new acts of magic to show your friends.

Just a piece of rope . . . something taken for granted by most of us. The builder of man's civilization, the tool without which modern industry would stop, life-line of the sailor, of the lumberman and of the adventure of mountains and the sky, the reason for the cowboy's being. Rope is all those things to all those people.

But it also is something to be used just for fun, the fun of Will Rogers' spinning ropes, of knots and crafts and legends, the sort of magic fun you can make for yourself, now that you know how, with just a piece of rope.

Rope Words

abaca—A form of banana plant grown mostly in the Philippines which provides fiber for manila rope. The botanical name for it is *Musa textilis*.

agave—A group of large cactus-like plants, the fiber of which is used to make sisal rope. Cantala fiber comes from the Agave Cantala plant of the Philippines and Dutch East Indies. Sisalana fiber is from the Agave Sisalana, grown in the East Indies, Africa and South America. Henequen is a fiber that comes from the Mexican plant Agave Four-croydes.

baler twine—A heavy binder twine for baling straw or hay by machine.

belay—Sailor's term for winding a rope around a cleat or pin so as to make the rope fast.

bell rope—A small hand rope attached to a bell so as to pull and ring it.

belly rope—Cowboy term for a roper's loop that slips over the shoulders of an animal and tightens around its belly as a result of using too large a loop in his lariat.

bend—A knot which ties two rope ends together. It comes from the same root word as *bind*.

bight—A loop or slack part of a rope, usually between the end and the standing part, made by bringing the end around near to or across itself.

binder twine—A single yarn, usually of hard fiber, used in harvesting for binding the sheaves.

bitter end—The last part of a working cable or rope.

block—A frame of wood or steel fitted with pulleys over which rope may be run to give added power for pulling or lifting things. When rigged with its rope, it is called a block and tackle.

body spin—A term used in rope spinning when a wide loop is spun up and over the head and then down around the body.

boom—A large, round heavy spar, pivoted at one end, usually for handling ship's cargo.

bos'n's chair—Also *bosun's chair* or *boatswain's chair*. A piece of board suspended from a rope as a seat for a man working aloft, so as to swing him up or down while he is painting or repairing, such as is used by a steeplejack.

braid—To interweave rope or cord or parts of it.

bull rope—A large rope used in oil well or gas well drilling and cleaning operations to transmit power from an engine.

butterfly—Usually the first trick in rope spinning. The roper starts his loop spinning in front of him or around his hand, enlarges the noose and spins it vertically and rapidly to the right and then left.

cable-laid—A rope made of three ropes of three standard strands each, all twisted left-handedly into a cable.

capstan—A revolving drum for winding in ropes in pulling or lifting.

cat line or *cathead line*—An oil well rope used for the power-hoisting of tools and pipe.

cheeks—The side pieces of the frame of a block.

Christmas tree twine—A single-ply twine, usually dyed green and treated with tar, for binding bundles of Christmas trees for shipping.

coil—A spiral of rope or a series of rings. As a verb, to lay down a rope in circular turns.

coir—The fiber from the outer husks of coconuts used to make a lightweight rope, usually in larger sizes or to be spliced into wire or manila lines to give them greater spring.

community loop—A cowboy's phrase for an extra-large lariat noose thrown by a roper to convey the idea that it would rope in the whole community. Also called a *cotton patch loop*.

cord—Small line made of several yarns.

cordage—The general term that covers all rope, cord, lines and string.

core—A small rope that runs through the center of a larger rope.

counter-clockwise—Left-handedly, in a direction opposite to the turning hands of a clock.

cow's tail—A frayed end of rope.

cracker—A short length of fiber drilling cable used in connection with a wire cable to give it more spring in oil well drilling.

double-banked rope—Sailor's term for a rope with men hauling on both sides.

end for end—To reverse a rope so as to use the opposite end.

eye—A spliced, seized or knotted loop, usually made in the end of a rope.

fake—One complete turn of a rope in a coil. The sailor calls it *flake*. A layer of such turns forms a *tier* and several layers, one on the other, form a *coil*.

fiber—Also often spelled fibre. The smallest threads of material which are twisted to make the yarns for rope or cord.

fid—A tapered hardwood pin used in working ropes, such as in separating the strands for splicing.

forefooting—A cowboy's roping of an animal by the forefeet.

fox—To twist yarns together in several ways.

ganging—A short commercial fishing line, attached at one end to a hook and at the other to a trawl or ground line. Gangings of from one to six feet long are attached along the trawl line at regular intervals.

going down the rope—A cowboy's term for approaching a roped animal, holding the rope taut as he goes toward it.

grab rope—A rope used as a handrail.

grind—A half-kink in a rope.

grommet—A ring or eyelet made of rope.

guy—A rope used for steadying or supporting something, such as a rope to strengthen an upright pole or the guy ropes which come out to the sides to help support a tent.

halyard—A line for hoisting sails or other things such as a flag on a pole.

hammer fall—A rope used on pile driving equipment to hoist the hammer to the derrick head. The rope is then released to drop the hammer so it pounds down on the pile.

hanging ropes—Fishermen's lines to which various sections of netting are hung so the lines will support the nets.

hank—A coil of cord consisting of a number of long turns covered with tight crossing turns.

hawser—Any large rope, at least five inches in circumference.

heart—The center of a rope, usually a slack-twisted rope or strand used as the core of another rope, especially as a fiber core in a wire rope.

heave—To haul in or pull on a line. Also to cast a *heaving line* ashore or to another vessel.

heel—Cowboy term meaning to rope an animal by the hind feet.

hemp—A plant grown in the United States and many other countries which gives a soft fiber. Formerly much used for making rope, but less so in recent years. Unlike the hard-fiber yielding perennials, hemp is an annual plant, the botanical name of which is *Cannabis sativa.* Now used mostly for small lines and high grade twines.

high-low—A rope spinner's term for a body spin which repeatedly raises and lowers the rope from the ground to as high as the performer can reach above his head. Also called *juggling.*

hitch—A way of securing a rope to an object or to another rope.

hooley-ann—A cowboy's way of swinging a loop of his lariat over the head of a horse to catch it in a corral with a single quick whirl.

hop-skip—When a rope spinner hops in and out of a vertical spinning noose.

horn—The part of a cowboy's saddle above the fork, technically called a *pommel,* which was a word the rancher never used.

hornswoggle—What a roped steer sometimes does to fool the cowboy by wriggling out of a rope so as to escape after being caught.

hurrah's nest—Sailor's term for a tangle of ropes and gear.

Irish pennant—The frayed or loose end of a line aboard ship, also slovenly rigging.

Jacob's ladder—A rope ladder, usually with wooden steps, hung over the side of a ship for the use of the pilot. Also called a *pilot's ladder.*

jam—To wedge rope tightly.

jerk line—A rope that was used to guide Western ox teams.

junk—Old rope or that saved to be salvaged by re-twisting and splicing.

jute—An annual plant grown mainly in India from which comes a soft fiber for rope, cordage, twine, burlap and many other uses.

knot—The forming of a knob in a rope by turning the rope on itself through a loop.

lanyard—An ornamental braid used to attach pocket knives, whistles and other small things.

lash—To bind two or more objects together with a rope, to wrap a single object with a series of turns or hitches, to secure any movable object so as to keep it from shifting position.

lay—As a verb, to twist strands together to form a rope. As a noun, the direction of the twist of a rope, the amount of turn put in it, or the angle of the strands. When the word is used to indicate tightness of the twist, rope usually is spoken of as being *hard-laid, medium-laid* or *soft-laid*. If something is done in a direction *with the lay* of a rope, it is in the direction in which the strands are twisted. *Against the lay* is the direction opposite the twist of the strands.

line—Common name for various kinds of cordage, especially aboard ship, referring to no specific kind.

loop—The bending of a rope to bring its sides toward each other or across.

maguey—The century plant, but a word the cowboy used to mean a hard rope made of its fiber, usually four-stranded.

manila—Rope made from abaca fiber, the main port of shipment for it being Manila in the Philippines. When used as the name of rope or fiber, it usually is spelled with a small "m" rather than with a capital letter. This is to indicate the type of material rather than the place, since not all manila fiber comes from Manila. However, you will see it spelled both ways.

marry—To bind two lines together temporarily.

mecate (may-cah'-tay)—A Mexican hair rope, often used by cowboys as a tie rope or reins, but seldom as a lariat.

messenger—A light rope used for hauling a heavier rope or a fuel line aboard a vessel.

middle a rope—To double it in such a way that both parts are equal in length.

mooring line—Rope used in docking a vessel or attached to the harbor anchor of yachts and smaller boats.

nip—The spot in a knot where the end is gripped to make it secure, also to grasp the end of a cord, as between the fingers or under the thumb.

ocean wave—A rope spinner's trick of flipping the noose back and forth in a wavy manner.

painter—A short rope fastened to the bow of a small boat to tie it up. A *sea painter* is a rope from the bow of a ship which is attached to a small boat so it can maneuver alongside the ship for landings, especially in rough weather.

pay out—To let a line run out or to let the slack out of it.

plain-laid—A rope in which three strands of left-handed yarn are twisted together to form a standard right-hand rope.

plat—To braid by interweaving rope or cord or parts of it. Also spelled *plait,* but usually pronounced the same as *plat.*

reef—To take in, especially to take in a sail or reduce its area.

reeve—To put the end of a rope through an eye or opening as through a block or a pulley.

ridge rope—The backbone rope of a tent or awning.

rogue's yarn—Colored strands woven into a rope to identify ownership.

roll—The wavelike motion the cowboy makes with a rope that whips along it to its end, sometimes used to release a lariat from a roped animal.

roll-over—When a rope spinner makes a spinning noose roll over his shoulders or arms.

rope—Strictly speaking, any cord of more than one inch circumference. However, most people except sailors call anything that isn't a string a rope, and that has become the common use of the word. Dictionaries accept the definition of rope as any twisting of fibers to make a large cord.

rope arm—The cowboy's right arm.

rope runner—A brakeman for mining equipment.

rope-yarn holiday—A half-holiday for a sailor, the free time supposed to be devoted to mending his clothes.

salt and pepper rope—A Western rope of alternating black and white horsehair.

seize—To bind a rope with small cord or yarn or to bind two ropes or two parts of the same rope together with a wrapping around of small cord.

sennit or *sinnet* or *synnet* or *sennet*—Braided cordage, usually of ornamental design.

shaking out—The cowboy's way of opening the noose of a lariat by giving it a few quick jerks toward the front while getting ready to throw it.

shoe sole rope—Cordage used in making rope-soled shoes.

shore line—The line used to fasten the inside end of a fisherman's net to shore to keep it in position while towing the outer end.

shovel rope—A line used to operate a shovel in the unloading of a grain boat.

sisal—One of the most-used kinds of rope. See *agave*.

skipping—A trick roping term for jumping in and out of a vertical spinning loop.

slack—The loose part of a rope or the part which hangs loosely between secured ends. The opposite of taut.

sling—A line passed around something so as to lift it or pull it, such as slinging some object that is to be hoisted. A lifting strap of rope.

splice—To join two parts of rope together by interweaving the ends or strands.

star gazing—When a rope spinner slowly sits down and then lies on his back, spinning all the while.

strand—Two or more yarns twisted together in the opposite direction to that of the yarn itself.

tackle—A combination of ropes and blocks for the purpose of increasing the pull.

taut—Tight, the opposite of slack.

tie-down rope—Used to secure aircraft, as in tying to the ground, for protection against wind in storms.

toggle—A small hardwood pin inserted into a knot to make it more secure or to allow for quick unfastening.

torpedo rope—Used to lower explosives into oil or gas wells.

trawl line—A long cord used by the fisherman, consisting of one or more coils of gear in a usually straight line with gangings attached at intervals.

trice—To pull taut or haul up a rope and secure it.

turn—A single winding of a rope.

unlay—To separate the strands of rope.

warp—A light hawser used to draw a vessel to a pier.

whip—To lash or seize the end of a rope to prevent it from fraying.

with the sun—In a clockwise or right-handed direction, the opposite of turning a rope *against the sun*.

yarn—Any number of individual threads or fibers twisted together.

~~~ *Some Books About Rope* ~~~

THERE are few books that deal with the whole subject of rope and its uses, but many have to do with some part of it. Listed here are some that will give the reader further information about things related to rope that may be of special interest:

THE STORY OF ROPES AND ROPEMAKING

Dickinson, H. W., *A Condensed History of Rope-making,* The New-comen Society for the Study of the History of Engineering and Technology, Transactions, Volume XXIII, 1942-3.

Edwards, H. T., *The Introduction of Abaca into the Western Hemisphere,* Publication 3831, The Smithsonian Institution, Washington, D.C.

Hopkins, J. F., *History of the Hemp Industry in Kentucky,* University of Kentucky Press, Lexington, Kentucky.

Morison, Samuel Eliot, *The Ropemakers of Plymouth,* Houghton Mifflin Company, Boston.

Ryder, David Warren, *Men of Rope,* Historical Publications, San Francisco.

Scherff, William A., *The Cordage Business,* Research Publishing Company, Boston.

Sprague, William B., *The Rope Maker,* Vol. II, Number 13, Chronicle of Early American Industries Association.

Weindling, Ludwig, *Long Vegetable Fibers,* Columbia University Press, New York.

―――, *Rope on the Farm,* U.S. Department of Agriculture, Farmers' Bulletin 2130, U.S. Government Printing Office, Washington, D.C.

―――, *Ropes and Rope-Making,* Men and Women at Work Series, Oxford University Press, London.

Some of the rope manufacturing companies have published manuals and booklets containing excellent general information. Among those which may be of interest to the average reader are:

Facts You Should Know About Cordage On Your Farm, Cordage Institute, New York.

Manual of Rope Usage, Plymouth Cordage Company, Plymouth, Massachusetts.

Rinek Rope, Rinek Rope Company, Easton, Pennsylvania.

Selection, Use and Care of Rope, Tubbs Cordage Company, San Francisco.

The Monument, A History of the Columbian Rope Company, Columbian Rope Company, Auburn, New York.

The Story of the United States Cordage Industry, Cordage Institute, New York.

Wall Rope, The Wall Rope Works, Inc., New York.

The background of the history, legends and uses of rope also is told in many books which are not written about rope itself. You may find some of these interesting for their stories and information:

Collier, John, *Indians of the Americas,* Mentor Books, New York.

Coxe, Antony, *A Seat at the Circus,* Evans Brothers, Ltd., London.

Dunbar, Seymour, *A History of Travel in America,* Tudor Publishing Company, New York.

Heffner, Hubert and Selden, Samuel; Hunton, Sellman, *Modern Theater Practice,* F. S. Crofts, New York.

La Farge, Oliver, *A Pictorial History of the American Indian,* Crown Publishers, New York.

Miller, John G., *Origins of the American Revolution,* Little, Brown & Company, Boston.

Sanders, Ruth, *The English Circus,* Werner Laurie, London.

Weeden, William B., *Economic and Social History of New England,* Houghton Mifflin Company, Boston.

————, *The Brooklyn Bridge,* Harper's New Monthly Magazine, May, 1883.

————, *Sailor Songs,* Harper's New Monthly Magazine, July, 1882.

————, *The Vertical Railway,* Harper's New Monthly Magazine, November, 1882.

KNOTS, PUZZLES, ROPE CRAFTS

Ashley, Clifford W., *The Ashley Book of Knots,* Doubleday and Company, Inc., Garden City, New York.

Burgess, J. Tom, *Knots, Ties and Splices,* George Routledge and Sons, London.

Cornell and Hoffman, *American Merchant Seaman's Manual,* Cornell Maritime Press.

Day, Cyrus Lawrence, *Sailors' Knots,* Dodd Mead and Company, New York.

Franklin, Eric, *Kamut, The Art of Making Pictures in String,* Academy of Recorded Crafts, Arts & Sciences, Croydon, England.

Graumont, Raoul and Hensel, John, *Encyclopedia of Knots and Fancy Rope Work,* Cornell Maritime Press, New York.

Griswold, Lester, *Handicraft,* Colorado Springs, Colorado.

Jaeger, Ellsworth, *Wildwood Wisdom,* The Macmillan Company, New York.

Jayne, Caroline, *String Figures,* Charles Scribner's Sons, New York.

Locke, L. Leland, *The Ancient Quipu or Peruvian Knot Record,* American Museum of Natural History, New York.

Lutz, Frank E., *String Figures from the Patomana Indians of British Guiana,* American Museum of Natural History, New York.

Thompson, Robert, *Rope Knots and Climbing,* U.S. Department of Interior, National Park Service, Tree Preservation booklet Number 7, Government Printing Office, Washington, D.C.

———, *Knots and Their Uses,* Tubbs Cordage Company, San Francisco.

———, *Knots That Everyone Should Know,* Great Western Cordage Company, Orange, California.

———, *Mastering the Art of Knots and Splices,* New Bedford Cordage Company, New Bedford, Massachusetts.

———, *Rope Knowledge for Riggers,* Columbian Rope Company, Auburn, New York.

COWBOY ROPES AND LARIATS

Croy, Homer, *Our Will Rogers,* Duell, Sloan & Pearce, Inc., New York.

Day, Donald, editor, *The Autobiography of Will Rogers,* Houghton Mifflin Company, Boston.

Dick, Everett, *The Story of the Frontier,* Tudor Publishing Company, New York.

Foster-Harris, *The Look of the Old West,* The Viking Press, New York.

Mason, Bernard S., *Roping,* A. S. Barnes & Company, New York.

Rogers, Betty, *Will Rogers, His Wife's Story,* Bobbs-Merrill Company, Indianapolis.

Rollins, Philip Ashton, *The Cowboy,* Charles Scribner's Sons, New York.

ROPE MAGIC

Hilliard, John Northern, *The Greater Magic Library,* A. S. Barnes & Company, New York.

Tarbell, Harlan, *Tarbell Course in Magic,* Louis Tannen, New York.

Varma, H. L., *The Indian Rope Trick,* The Society of Indian Magicians, Bombay.

———, *Abbott's Encyclopedia of Rope Tricks,* Abbott's Magic Novelty Company, Colon, Michigan.

Index